HOW TO
INVEST
YOUR MONEY

HAMLYN HELP YOURSELF GUIDE

HOW TO INVEST YOUR MONEY

JOHN MORGAN

HAMLYN

To Alison Mills, my father Jack Morgan,
and Anthony Swanston of Towry Law Group, for their help
and support in this project.

First published in 1990 by
The Hamlyn Publishing Group Limited
a division of the Octopus Publishing Group
Michelin House, 81 Fulham Road,
London SW3 6RB

ISBN 0 600 56900 4

Printed in and bound in Great Britain by Collins, Glasgow.

CONTENTS

Introduction   9

1. Getting to Grips with Investing   12
Can I afford to invest?   12
You pay before you invest   13
So how should we spend our money?   13
How to budget successfully   14
Now can we invest?   14
Why do you want to invest?   15
What strategy best suits me?   16

2. My First Investment — (and I Didn't Even Know It!)   19
Living with wealth   19
But what about the downside?   20
What is a mortgage? – Can I afford one?   20
Safe or risky mortgages?   21
Flexibility is important!   23
Taxation – the 'MIRAS effect'   24
The ups and downs of interest rates   25
Investing via home improvements   26
Protecting your investment   27
Raising money from your home   27

3. Taxation and the Investor   29

Understanding tax is important when saving
and investing   29
Investing under independent taxation   31
Too much income – a problem for pensioners?   32
Gross income versus net income   32
Will I ever pay capital gains tax?   33
And what about inheritance tax?   35

4. Banking Your Cash   37

The current account revolution   37
Investing with your current account   38
Getting your cash from A to B   39
But what about my savings?   40
So which account should I choose?   41
What do the banks have to offer?   42
And what about the building societies?   44

5. Investing – How to avoid losing your shirt!   46

So you want to play safe?   46
Setting out your objectives   48
Investor protection and the Financial Services Act   50
Where to seek advice   52

6. National Savings   55

An ideal investment for the big and the small   55
Yearly Plan – guaranteed return in a
fluctuating world   56
Ordinary account – an account for the kids?   58
Investment account – the children's choice   59
Savings certificates – fixed-interest or index-linked?   59
Income bonds – ideal for non-taxpayers   60
Capital bonds – a capital idea?   61
Taking a gamble – Premium Bonds   61

7. Life Assurance   63

Investment or protection?   63
With profits and unit-linked   64
Why invest in life assurance?   67
But what about annuities?   69

8. Pensions   71

One of the better investments?   71
So what are the choices?   72
The pros and cons of the company scheme   73
Why invest the company way?   74
Personal pensions – a viable alternative?   76
SERPS was revolutionized too!   77
Boosting your pension – more changes   77
What happens if I retire early or change jobs?   78
Pensions – seek advice!   79

9. The Stock Market   80

A different sort of risk!   80
Are we ready to invest?   81
What do I want from my investment – the case for gilts?   82
Let's buy shares – the case for collective investments   85

10 Unit Trusts   88

So what is so good about unit trusts?   88
How do unit trusts work?   88
How unit trusts provide an income   89
How do I choose?   91
How to buy and sell units   93
What about tax?   95
Lump sum, savings plans and portfolios   95
Unit trusts vs the rest   96

11 Investment Trusts 98

A better deal for your money? 98
How do investment trusts work? 100
How do investment trusts provide an income? 100
Seek help when choosing an investment trust 102
What about taxation? 103
Investment trusts vs the rest 104

12 Raising the Stakes – Investing in Shares 106

Risk and reward 106
How to reduce the risks 108
Looking for a bargain 109
Watching the market 112
Buying and selling 114

13. Personal Equity Plans 116

Stock market investments – tax and the PEPs revolution 116
So what is a PEP? 117
Why put PEP into your investments? 118

14. Higher Risk Investments 121

Options 121
The Business Expansion Scheme 122
The Unlisted Securities Market – and others 125

Useful Addresses 126

Introduction

Investing is a matter a judgement. Good judgement is gleaned from knowledge, and knowledge can be gleaned from this book.

This 'Help Yourself Guide' is by no means a heavyweight reference book – rather it is aimed at generating interest in what many might feel to be a seemingly impenetrable subject.

As a financial journalist I receive hundreds of letters each year concerning a wide range of investment matters from a wide variety of people – the wealthy, those less well-off, the elderly, young people, and from those in middle age.

It never ceases to surprise me that even the most educated – those with the most sophisticated investments – often have little knowledge of how they work, or indeed, how they 'fit' into a general individual investment strategy.

I hope that this book will enable you to put your investments into perspective, to enable you to sort out your priorities, to appreciate risk, rather than be frightened of it.

On the whole, successful investment is not difficult to achieve. What is difficult is the ability to make up your mind exactly what you want from your investment and what level of risk is acceptable to you.

Even the basic principles are not difficult to grasp. Indeed, in many respects investing is like gardening.

In gardening you prepare the ground, tend your crop, and reap the harvest. Investing involves the same process. You have to prepare your ground carefully, monitor your investment closely, and when it matures you take the spoils.

And, like gardening, you have to approach your subject in the right way. If the gardener does not prepare his ground properly, if he or she chooses bad plants, if they are sited in the wrong place, if the plants are not nurtured, then even the most green-fingered practitioner could not expect a decent crop.

And so it is with the investor. The fact is that if you do not take an active interest, then you cannot expect to become a proficient investor, and you certainly cannot expect to do as well as your neighbour.

Yes, you can find investment products that need less 'tending' than others, products which are less risky, but these are the same investments which give a lower return, and low returns in themselves should be regarded as risky.

Let's get one thing straight – it is not difficult to invest. Much of it is to do with common sense and the grasping of basic principles. Neither does it mean being over cautious – far from it. Careful investment means applying yourself energetically to the issues at hand.

And it is only once you have established what you are trying to achieve from a given position that you can move forward and invest successfully.

You can only achieve your objectives if you know where you stand before taking the plunge, and this book hopes to help you do that.

Perhaps more importantly it also looks at the unknown factor – the element of 'risk'.

No gardener worth his salt would simply plant a dozen tomato plants in his garden in the hope that they will yield a bumper crop. The risks have to reduced by planting in a glasshouse, protecting through spraying against infestation, and nurturing through feeding.

The expert tomato grower knows that the level of investment needed to grow a decent crop in a greenhouse is high, but he is also aware that the risk of failure is reduced when planting under glass.

There are products which are less risky than others. However, all investments – even the humble building society deposit account – carry a degree of risk.

Because those who take the greatest risk stand to reap the

greatest reward, people will take chances. Hopefully, however, by the time you have finished reading this book you will have an understanding of how to reduce your exposure to risk.

The key to successful investment is understanding – these following pages are designed to give you that understanding.

ONE

Getting to Grips with Investing

Can I afford to invest?

It might seem a simple question, but many people either do not know whether they can afford to invest or are not sure at which point they start investing.

It is perhaps not surprising in today's environment when you even have to think carefully about whether your nest egg in the building society represents your savings or your investment.

So let us start by accepting that 'saving' means putting money aside out of your income to cover some eventuality, be it to buy a new car or furniture, or simply to be salted away for a 'rainy day'.

Given that you can get interest on your savings if you deposit them with a bank or building society, your savings become an 'investment' simply because, given that they are in the right sort of account, that institution pays you interest – it gives you a 'return on capital'.

Once you seek a return on your investment, then you become an 'investor' and serious investors, even with the humble building society deposit account, can make more money than those who cannot be bothered.

That might be the difference between 'saving' and 'investing', but in describing these differences I have used another term which is often misunderstood, and that is the term 'income'.

Again it might seem a straightforward concept, but many

people tend to forget that income means more than your pay cheque at the end of the week.

For our purposes then, 'income' can be described as money that is earned either through our job or our investments.

The taxman does not discriminate between whether your last pound was earned from your job or from your building society. As far as he is concerned it is all 'income'.

You pay before you invest

Before you can even think of saving or investing you have to recognize that there are costs which have to be borne out of income. For most of us, the Government becomes the first creditor, dipping as it does into our income, to obtain our taxes.

It is therefore fundamental that we have a basic grasp of tax matters, if we are to invest properly, if only to make sure that we use the tax system to our best advantage.

Tax is not all that the Government takes from us. It also takes National Insurance contributions, but unlike tax, NI contributions are more difficult to manipulate to our best advantage. So for investment purposes, other than noting the hole left in our pay packets when NI is deducted, let us forget about it.

So where does that leave us potential investors? That hole left by deductions from our salaries is important because what money is left for us to spend is our 'net income'.

It is important to grasp the difference between 'net income' and income earned before the Government's deductions, that is, our 'gross income', because this, too, is of fundamental importance to the potential investor.

So how should we spend our money?

That is one question which I am sure you know the answer to already. The fact is we all have to pay for the basic necessities of life, be they lighting, heating, clothing or food, and we all like to have some left over for less essential items – the car, entertainment, reading etc.

But knowing how to spend money is important if we are to

become investors. Budgeting is important to the investor, if only to ensure that you will have enough money left over to invest.

Most of you seasoned investors would realize that I might be stating the obvious; after all, you cannot save what you do not have. But budgeting is about ensuring you keep track of your money, and that discipline is essential when investing.

As I said in my Introduction, investing is like gardening. Investments must be carefully monitored – weekly, monthly and annually.

How to budget successfully

First, you need to add together all your sources of income – your pay, the interest received from your savings, any social security payments – and then deduct from them your outgoings.

As you can now pay for any regular bill on a monthly basis, you could try to get to grips with paying by standing order or direct debit from your current account.

For many people, this is a useful way of spreading the cost of bills throughout the year. And providing you monitor your bill payments carefully, then you should be able to manage a steady outflow of funds.

You can even save part of your income, to pay the annual bills – those that cannot be spread throughout the year, such as your car tax or your club membership.

Having done all that, you will be left with a sum of money which can be spent on other necessities such as food and clothing. You should be able to estimate roughly how much you have to spend on each, and take that into account when doing your budget.

Now can we invest?

Not really. You still have to budget for the pleasures of life – spending on fashion, new furniture, the car, the cinema, restaurants etc. Only once you have allowed yourself a proportion of your income for such spending, can you even begin to start thinking of investing.

So now can I invest? Possibly. But before you go forward ask yourself this question: have you remembered to 'protect' yourself and your family? Part of your budgeting must include adequate insurance protection just in case the unexpected occurs.

What happens if your roof blows off in a storm? What happens if you have to take time off work through illness? What happens when you retire? What happens if you die?

If you have not catered for these eventualities, your whole investment strategy could go the same way as your roof or flooded living room. *It is a golden rule that you must ensure that you are adequately protected before putting money into investments.*

Insurance, by the way, represents another bill which can successfully be taken into account when doing your budget.

It should be said at this point that insurance is an unusual animal in the sense that it can also be regarded as an important investment. There is more about this in Chapter Seven where I discuss insurance at greater length.

Suffice it to say that while insurance can be an investment, so too can investments be regarded as an insurance. Indeed, the very nature of saving can be regarded as a kind of insurance – that is why we say we are 'saving for a rainy day'.

Why do you want to invest?

Everyone has different reasons for wishing to invest. It might be that you want to improve your home or to buy a car; equally, it could be that you want a lump sum to buy a second home, or you might want to increase your income, either in the future or now.

All these reasons might lead you to invest. The question is, what sort of strategy will achieve your objective?

Adopting a strategy – deciding what you want to achieve – is central to investment. It does not matter whether you are a prince or a pauper, the fact is you have to decide what you want to do with your money.

The strategy for investing for a set period of say two years – perhaps for a deposit for a house or a new car – is very different from the strategy of 'saving for a rainy day'.

And no two investors are the same. The investment strategy of an 18-year-old is not likely to be the same as one for a 30-, 50-, 60- or 80-year-old, even though their income may be exactly the same. What use investing in a pension scheme if you have reached the grand old age of 80? Indeed, what use a pension scheme if you are just 16 years old?

What strategy best suits me?

The strategy which you are likely to adopt will almost certainly stem from your desire to reduce risk, and this, in turn, is most likely to stem from the desire not to risk what hard-earned cash you have set aside, or are likely to set aside, to invest.

And the strategy will be dictated by personal circumstances. An elderly person's strategy will differ from a younger person's, a taxpayer's strategy will differ from the non-taxpayer's, the poorer person's strategy will differ from the wealthy person's.

Bearing this in mind then, let us look at six strategies where the level of risk increases according to circumstances. It does not matter at the moment what the investments actually are – we will look at those in later chapters – rather, let us look at the principles underlying the six strategies.

The first strategy is for the cautious investor. It does not matter whether our Mr Very Cautious is a young man, a middle-aged man or, indeed, a senior citizen.

Suffice it to say that he has a relatively small sum of money to invest, and that he wants to invest it where, without fuss, he can easily get his hands on it – all while gaining interest to help boost his total 'income'. Mr Cautious is therefore looking at what is generally regarded as a 'safe' investment.

Such a strategy lends itself naturally to certain investment products – products which I will go into more thoroughly later in this book.

The second strategy is for someone who also regards himself as cautious, but slightly less so than his brother Mr Very Cautious. Mr Less Cautious wants his money to have a high level of security, but gains a higher level of 'income' from the invested capital. Mr Less Cautious wants the prospect of higher rates and, like his brother, wants to invest relatively small amounts. In order to achieve higher rates he invests in products which may be of higher risk or simply less accessible than those used by Mr Very Cautious.

In this case, Mr Less Cautious's investment strategy may lead him to invest in similar products to Mr Very Cautious or they could be quite different.

Our third strategy involves a third brother, Mr Quite Cautious. Mr Quite Cautious wants to keep his capital safe but he wants to go for even more growth in interest. And he would not mind taking a greater risk to see his capital grow in value.

Mr Quite Cautious's strategy could then well lead him to invest in quite different investments from his two brothers.

Our fourth strategy is adopted by Mr Average Risk. Like his friends, Mr Average Risk is careful with his money, but because he is better-off than all the Cautious brothers, he wants to stick his neck out a bit further and so he wants to invest in products designed to balance high returns with high growth and high security.

That might seem impossible, but Mr Average Risk's strategy is, in fact, more susceptible to risk than his three neighbours'. Again, his strategy determines the type of investment open to him particularly as he can afford to take greater risks.

Mr Average Risk's brother, Mr Greater Risk, is so well-off that he needs someone else to manage his money. He is prepared to pay more to achieve this end, and is prepared to allow his managers to take greater risks.

The fifth strategy, therefore, is quite different from all the others that have come before, and it is quite different from the sixth and final strategy.

Mr Variable Risk is saving for a fixed period of time. His strategy is therefore designed to be initially risky, and then become more safe as time goes on so that when he comes to take his profits, he will not find that a sudden downturn has hit his accrued returns too severely.

Now that you can afford to invest – all your bills are paid,

you have decided on your priorities, you can budget successfully, you have worked out a strategy – what is left?

You need to work out what to invest in, and indeed take
into account your existing investments – some of which you
might not even be aware of.

TWO

My First Investment – (And I Didn't Even Know It!)

Living with wealth

Your home not only provides a roof over your head, but can be regarded as the greatest investment you are likely to make in your life, thanks to the huge rise experienced in house values in recent years.

If you take the recent period, between 1985 and 1989, house prices increased sharply, rising on average by around 22.8 per cent per year.

Contrast that with the average rate of inflation in that period, which was around 5.1 per cent.

The growth of house price values has been enormous. In 1956 the average house price was £2,230; this has risen, sometimes quickly, sometimes very slowly, to a position where the same house would now be worth around £65,512 – a quite startling increase.

So for those of you who bought your house in the 1950s, 'sixties and 'seventies, you could well be sitting on a small fortune – and it is a fortune which can be used if you so wish to achieve certain investment objectives.

For example, you can use this hidden wealth to help raise money from your home in order to provide an income, or you can use it to improve your home – but I shall be saying more about this later.

But what about the downside?

There is no doubt, then, that the housing market has been a good place to 'invest'. Not only do you provide a roof over your head but you potentially also have a good investment in the longer term.

But, as with many investments, the housing market is a cyclical one in that some years house price inflation rises quickly while in others its rises slowly or even falls.

Indeed, while the prices of houses in estate agents' windows have generally always increased year in year out, in real terms – when inflation is taken into account – house price values actually fell in the years between 1974 and 1977 and again between 1980 and 1982.

Yet despite these cyclical downturns, the dual nature of property – to provide a roof over your head and act as an investment – still makes it an attractive option for the first-time investor.

What is a mortgage? – can I afford one?

Sadly, not everyone can afford to buy. The same house price inflation that has made many people relatively wealthy has pushed the cost of housing beyond the reach of many hopeful buyers.

Most people nowadays need to borrow money in order to buy their home, and this is usually done through a 'mortgage' – but there is more to the humble mortgage than meets the eye from the investor's point of view.

It has become customary – and quite wrongly so – that the homeloan and the life assurance covering it are regarded as one, and are packaged as such. This is particularly so with endowment mortgages, which will be explained later.

You should take a more discerning view of mortgages so that when you need one you will get what you want and not that which the lender wants to sell you!

The borrowing process involves three principle elements. There is the 'loan', which I shall describe as the 'capital element', which pays for your new property. Then we have the 'interest' – this represents the cost of financing the loan, a cost which you have to pay. And finally, we have the 'insurance' – the life assurance which most lenders require in order to ensure that if anything happens to you, then they can get their money back from your estate without the bother of selling your property.

There is no overriding reason why you the investor should have to accept all three elements in one package without taking a closer look at what you are getting.

Indeed, these days, there is no reason why one organization should not provide the loan – without seeking repayment of the capital, while another could be used as a savings medium so that you can pay off the loan in the longer term, and a third institution could then provide the insurance.

Safe or risky mortgages?

Well, let us look at the types of mortgage available to fund the loan on our investment and I will try to assess the risks involved in each type.

The two most common types of mortgage these days are the 'repayment mortgage' and the 'endowment mortgage', both of which come in different forms with different names, and you need to seek further advice on them should you need one.

These two types of mortgage are fundamentally different in ways which are important for you the investor to understand.

Put simply, the repayment mortgage is a loan on which both capital and interest are repaid over a period of time – usually 25 years.

Apart from the actual repayment mortgage most lenders also insist that you take out life assurance so that they can retrieve the loan from your estate should you die.

The endowment method is quite different. An endowment is a loan on which only the interest is paid during the life of the mortgage. The capital – the actual loan – is covered by investing money in an insurance company savings scheme. At the end of 25 years, you should have enough money saved to pay off the original loan.

Because you invested in an insurance company's savings

scheme you automatically have the benefit of life assurance.

Both schemes have the advantages of being 'low risk'. The very nature of the repayment mortgage guarantees that the loan is repaid – providing of course you keep up the monthly premiums over the course of the mortgage.

The endowment mortgage also guarantees repayment of the loan but only if you die.

However, the risk of the mortgage not being covered after 25 years is reduced substantially because the endowment mortgage is a savings plan – an investment in its own right. Hopefully, then the amount actually accrued over the period of the loan could well exceed the size of the loan, leaving the happy investor with a lump sum and no mortgage.

For the cautious investor, the endowment mortgage therefore appears to offer the ideal balance between risk and reward, as historically the loan has always been covered by the endowment's accrued bonuses.

Unfortunately, there is more to it than that. Remember the three elements of the mortgage – the capital, the interest and the insurance.

By 'unbundling' these three elements, you the investor, potentially could do much better, simply because unbundling enables you to choose your own savings plan – a plan which hopefully will perform much better than the endowment savings plan offered by the insurance company.

Unit trusts and Personal Equity Plans (PEPs) will be explained in much greater detail in chapters 10 and 13 respectively. However, you should be aware at this point that by choosing a new type of mortgage linked to a PEP you could do much better than investing through a repayment or an endowment.

These new-style plans are potentially more risky than the safer endowment mortgage, but also, they could do much better. As I will say a number of times during the course of this book, *'the greater the risk the greater the reward'*.

But how great is this risk? To answer that we can only look back to what happened in the past, and what would have happened if unit-trust-only PEP mortgages had been available.

What happened in the past does not guarantee future performance, but it does serve as probably the best guide available to us.

If, as a 30-year-old, you had 25 years ago taken out a basic 'with-profits' endowment mortgage paying £30 a month to the best performing company – the giant Scottish-based insurance company Standard Life – your investment would now be worth around £57,923, which is probably more than enough to pay off your homeloan.

However, if you had invested the same amount in the best performing unit trust in the UK General sector – M&G's Midland and General Trust – your savings plan would now be worth £152,264 – considerably more than the endowment mortgage.

With the advent of the new tax-saving vehicle which can be attached to unit trust investments – the Personal Equity Plan – because gross rather than net income is reinvested, that figure would have been even higher.

Even if we take the average UK- invested unit trust versus the average endowment, there is no contest – the unit trust wins hands down, with a 'payout' of £86,126 against the average endowment of £43,911.

The point, and it is fundamental to investing, is that *the longer you invest your money, the less risk is involved*. A 25-year mortgage, therefore, is an ideal period to iron-out risk.

Flexibility is important!

But there is more to performance than simply accruing a huge sum of money after 25 years of paying a mortgage.

'Flexibility' is of fundamental importance to the investor. What happens, for example, if you are merrily paying off your mortgage and you suddenly inherit £50,000 – enough to pay off your loan.

With a repayment mortgage there is no problem. If you wish, you simply send a cheque to your lender and pay off your mortgage – though for reasons I shall explain in a moment, that is not always the investor's best option.

You can also pay off the loan with an endowment mortgage, but that leaves you with the savings plan which, with most companies, has to be retained for a set period – often 25 years. You can surrender your policy and take your savings out, but that is fraught with problems because you are often penalized heavily for doing so.

Indeed, in the early years of an endowment savings plan your policy might not be worth anything despite your having contributed for one, two or three years. This is because the insurance company often pays such high commissions to the person who sold you the policy – usually a bank or building society – that you are forced to continue paying into your savings scheme even though it might not be appropriate to your changed circumstances.

Another option would be to freeze payments into the policy, but you still have to wait until maturity before you can get your hands on your money.

The 'riskier' unit-trust-only PEP mortgage does not have this problem because it is more flexible. The unit trust savings plan can be stopped and started as often as you wish.

Incidentally, the charges are easier to identify with these new mortgages because some are made when the policy is set up while others are deducted at a set rate each year.

Taxation – the 'MIRAS effect'

Another aspect of mortgages and buying your home is taxation. The mortgage holder can get tax relief on the first £30,000 of the loan.

This effectively cuts the amount you pay out each month by whatever proportion taxation is to the pound. So if tax is, say, 25p in the pound, then your outgoings to your mortgage lender are reduced by 25p for every £1 paid over in premium.

For the majority of people the 'discounted' rate is worked out at source by your lender under the 'Mortgage Interest Relief at Source' scheme – otherwise known as MIRAS.

You should be aware of this tax relief because it has a bearing on how you arrange your investments. Take the case outlined above of someone inheriting £50,000.

If the investor's mortgage is £50,000, it might be better to pay off £20,000 of the mortgage – the £20,000 which does not attract tax relief, and maintain the homeloan at £30,000.

This then enables the smart investor to invest the rest of his inheritance in something else. If you wish to do this you have to make sure that the investment you choose performs well and out-paces the interest you pay on your remaining mortgage after tax relief.

In other words, if your £30,000 mortgage costs say £250 per month at prevailing interest rates, then the £30,000 balance of your inheritance needs to make more than £250 per month if you are to come out on top – and there is no reason, if you invest wisely, why this should not be the case.

The ups and downs of interest rates

Interest rates vary up and down. You can buy a house and the loan costs nine per cent one month, then the rate soars to 14 per cent a few months later.

This roller coaster has to be managed effectively through your budgeting, and you should always be aware, particularly when interest rates are low, that they can always rise again leaving you to find more cash than may be available.

Schemes are available to help iron out the fluctuations in interest rates, but be careful in choosing one, particularly those which defer payments over long periods.

A good lender will be prepared to lend around 2½ times the level of your income, and add the value of your partner's income. However, in recent years this ratio has been increased to three or even four times income, which can seriously damage your financial health when interest rates rise.

As we shall see later, interest rates also have to be managed carefully when investing in a property because high interest rates can depress demand and that, in turn, depresses house price inflation. If that happens then you could find that you are funding a high-interest-rate mortgage for extended periods while house values are falling in real terms.

High interest rates are also bad news when investment returns begin to dip. It is possible that it becomes a better tack to pay off your mortgage than maintain one when interest rates are high and the return from other investments is low.

Investing via home improvements

Home improvements are a good way of increasing the value of your main investment – your home – as well as making your property a better place in which to live.

However, you should be careful as to which 'improvements' you undertake. Some so-called 'improvements' such as stone cladding, may actually reduce the value of your home, while others may not, in investment terms, be worth undertaking.

The Woolwich Building Society does a regular survey looking at the top ten most popular improvements and gives some idea of how much of your outlay on home improvements is likely to be recouped when the house is sold.

The following table illustrates the point:

- **Annual Maintenance** – 100 per cent recouped.
- **Central Heating** – Most if not all recouped.
- **Extensions** – 'Reasonable' extensions: most cost recouped.
- **Loft Conversions** – 80 per cent recouped.
- **Kitchens** – 50 to 60 per cent recouped
- **Bathrooms** – Basic bathrooms, most of cost recouped
- **Gardens** – Heavy investment, unlikely to recoup cost
- **Internal decor** – 100 per cent recouped if not elaborate
- **Insulation/energy conservation measures** – Basic costs yes, double glazing and cavity wall filling, no.

It does not matter what you do to some houses, their ultimate value will be capped by the local market conditions. The value of improved houses will always be pegged by the cost of similar houses in the same area – so be careful when improving.

Improving an underdeveloped house – one which appears cheap when compared to like houses within its locality – can improve its value substantially and is therefore a good investment.

Such improvements can be paid for by extending your

existing mortgage – a process made much easier where the value of your home far exceeds the current level of your loan.

However, from a pure investment point of view, you must make sure that the improvement to your home does result in a corresponding rise in value.

Protecting your investment

You must protect your home and, for that matter, its contents by taking out adequate insurance.

You can shop around for the best deals by going to an insurance broker. Unlike your mortgage lender, who might be interested in offering the choice of one or just a handful of companies, a broker can provide you with the best deal available for the least cost. The same applies to insuring the contents of your home.

Then there is the question of insuring your life. We have already seen that mortgage lenders often insist on your taking out a mortgage protection policy so that they know that your estate will have money to cover their loan should you die.

Now you need to ensure that you have life assurance in order to protect the interests of your family – your husband or wife and your children.

The sale of life assurance is now highly regulated, so see Chapter 5 for a few pointers about from whom you should buy it.

Raising money from your home

At the outset of this chapter I said that houses are a good investment and that many people now have a valuable property often without the millstone of a mortgage.

That valuable property can now be used to achieve some useful investment objectives. This value, hidden in bricks and mortar, can be used to raise cheap cash in order to buy other investments to fulfil changing needs.

For example, elderly people often live in an expensive house but have very little income to maintain it – they are known as 'house rich – cash poor'.

By releasing equity in their homes they can now gain an income. So how is this achieved?

There are two main schemes, Home Income Schemes and Home Reversion Schemes, and both need to be treated with extreme caution.

Home Income Schemes work by taking a mortgage out on part of the value of your property and investing the money into an annuity which guarantees an income. That then enables you to pay the mortgage premiums, leaving some money over to boost your income.

Such schemes are ideal for more elderly citizens because the annuity rates – the amount actually paid out in income – is higher the older you are, and men get more than woman at the same age because they are not expected to live as long.

The Home Reversion Scheme is different in that you sell your home to a company which allows you to stay living in the property, often rent-free.

In this case the company offering the scheme simply gives you a lump sum which can be used, if you wish, to buy an annuity.

While both schemes can prove to be excellent investments I would strongly urge you to seek expert advice. Before going that far, get hold of a copy of Age Concern's booklet, 'Using Your Home as Capital' and read it thoroughly. You may obtain the booklet, which cost £2.50, from Age Concern England, 60 Pitcairn Road, Mitcham, Surrey CR4 3LL.

THREE

Taxation and the Investor

Why understanding tax is important when saving and investing

You need a working knowledge of taxation – at least the basic principles – if you want to delve seriously into the world of investment.

There are three main taxes to consider – income tax, capital gains tax and inheritance tax.

Any one or more of these taxes could have a fundamental bearing on your investment strategy.

One of the basic rules of investing is that you should always try to reduce the amount of tax paid in order to maximize your investment returns.

Let us look at income tax first. Just as there are three main taxes to consider, there are also three main types of income tax payer, the difference between each of them being that some are non-taxpayers, others are basic rate taxpayers, and the rest are higher rate taxpayers.

The category in which you fall determines the type of investment you should go into. This does not mean that each group is mutually exclusive. Certain investment products from the Government's own Department of National Savings, for example, are worthwhile for non-taxpayers and higher rate taxpayers, but not for basic rate taxpayers. There will be more about National Savings in Chapter 6.

Of course the main determining factor as to which category you fall into is 'income'. As I have said before, the Inland Revenue regards income as not only your earnings from employment, but also from investments.

Calculating 'taxable income' therefore is relatively straight-forward – you simply add up all your 'gross' earnings and any investment income on which tax has not already been paid. You have to add in some state benefits you may be receiving, but not others.

In fact, the majority of investments have tax deducted at source – the main popular exceptions again being certain National Savings products – so that as a basic rate taxpayer you need do nothing.

So now that you know your gross income you can find out into which category of income taxpayer you fall.

The first thing to remember is that you do not pay tax on all your gross income. All of us have allowances which, subject to our status, have to be deducted from our gross annual salary figure.

Married people get a bigger allowance and so pay less tax than single people. Elderly people have a larger allowance than younger people, and the very old have larger allowances than those who have just retired.

For example, in the 1989-90 tax year, single people got an allowance of £2,785 and the married personal allowance was £4,375.

So just as tax allowances separate the taxpayer from the non-taxpayer, the upper income threshold separates the basic rate taxpayer from the higher rate taxpayer.

In the 1989-90 tax year, anyone earning more than £20,700 becomes a higher rate taxpayer, while those taxpayers below this threshold are basic rate taxpayers.

Those who reach the state retirement age of 60 for women and 65 for men are then awarded the 'age allowance'. The single age allowance in the 1989-90 tax year is £3,400 and £5,385 if you are married. The allowance begins to be reduced once your income exceeds £11,400.

There is also a special allowance for those aged 75 and over. The single 75 plus allowance is £3,540 while the married allowance is £5,565.

30

Investing under independent taxation

The 1989-90 tax year was also a significant one because it was the last tax year when husbands and wives were regarded as one person, for taxation purposes.

Hitherto, the husband had to account for their taxation to the Inland Revenue and the wife's income from employment was added to his earned income. Tax was deducted once 'his' allowances were taken into account.

Any income from investments which might be owned by the wife was also treated as the husband's income – a poor state of affairs when that same woman might not be working and might otherwise have been a non-taxpayer.

All that changes in 1990-91 when independent assessment is introduced. This is a much more equitable way of working out income tax as each individual, regardless of whether they are married, is regarded independently as a taxpayer.

This also has fundamental implications for the investor. For example, if a wife is not in salaried employment but receives income from investments, then it stands to reason that she should make best use of her allowances.

What I mean is this. If the wife is able to get the income from investments paid gross then she can earn as much as she likes up to her tax threshold before she has to pay any tax.

It stands to reason, therefore, that if a wife is not earning an income and the husband has some investments, then he should transfer some of those investments into her name so that she can make best use of her allowances, and the husband and wife investment team pays less tax overall!

Providing they can either get income from investments paid gross, or at least reclaim tax paid on those investments, they are making the best use of their allowances under independent assessment.

Another wheeze worth noting is that if the wife is a taxpayer, but the husband is on low income, then the unused part of the married couple's allowance – which he would normally claim – can be transferred to the wife. In the 1990-91 tax year a special arrangement allows the transfer of the unused part of the man's personal allowance – this will not be the case in future years, except in certain cases.

Elderly married couples also need to take account of independent taxation, particularly as there are special rules to ensure that the changes do not leave some couples actually less well off as a result of the changes in 1990-91.

On all tax matters, including independent taxation, the Inland Revenue produces some good leaflets. On this particular matter, 'IR80: Independent Taxation: A Guide for Married Couples', 'IR81: Independent Taxation: A Guide for Pensioners' and 'IR82: Independent Taxation: A Guide for Husbands on a Low Income' are all leaflets which are worth reading. They should all be available from local tax offices.

Too much income – a problem for pensioners?

You probably think that you cannot have too much income. However, for many elderly people a reasonable income in old age does create some income tax problems of which the keen investor should be aware.

In particular, there is the once notorious 'age allowance trap'. Nowadays this once horrendous anomaly has largely disappeared, but the remnants of the problem still remain.

It works like this. Age allowance is 'capped' and gradually reduced when income exceeds £11,400, by £1 for every £2 of income. This means that the benefit disappears once income reaches £12,630 for single people and £13,420 for married couples in the 1989-90 tax year.

Older investors, therefore, have to take this into account when the income from their investment begins to knock on the age trap door.

Gross income versus net income

I have already mentioned the need for non-taxpaying investors to search for gross investment income – that is income which is either not taxed or from which the tax can be reclaimed from the Inland Revenue, in the context of independent taxation.

And I have also mentioned the fact that some investments might be liked by non-taxpayers and higher rate taxpayers, but not by basic rate taxpayers.

Well, the fact is that the investor must be fully aware of whether his investment pays gross income – or potentially gross income – and net income.

For example, a non-taxpayer should not necessarily put money into a bank or building society account because he cannot claim back the tax which has been taken out of the interest paid to him at source.

However, that same non-taxpayer may hold some shares, and the income generated by those shares is also paid tax deducted. However, in this case, the non-taxpayer can claim back the tax paid.

Tax-free investments are another matter. All winnings on Premium Bonds are not taxed. This is particularly appealing to the higher rate taxpayer because the value of his 'winnings' – his return on his investment – is effectively greater than when the non-taxpayer wins.

This is because income from any normal taxable investment would be reduced by 40 per cent for the higher rate taxpayer, by 25 per cent for the basic rate taxpayer, and not at all for the non-taxpayer.

Will I ever pay capital gains tax?

So far under this section I have been discussing the tax you pay on investment income. Capital gains tax – known as CGT – is a tax on the growth of investment capital.

It stands to reason, therefore, that as an investor, you need to get clear in your mind the difference between income and capital.

Suffice it to say that investment income is the money earned from capital in the shape of interest on deposits, such as the interest you get from a building society account or the dividend paid from shares, while the growth in capital is the growth in the value of that investment.

While you might get a regular income from a building society deposit in the shape of interest, the capital invested

33

with the building society will never grow.

This is not the case with shares, where the income might increase, as might the value of the shares resulting in capital growth. It is this capital growth which may be subject to capital gains tax.

Perhaps a simpler example of capital growth is with a painting. If you buy a painting in a boot sale for £10 and then sell it for £100, then you have 'realized' a capital gain.

It is only when you 'transfer' an item – usually by selling it – that the capital gain occurs. Even then you might not have to pay the CGT.

So how do you know when you have to pay? First of all, as with income tax, everyone has an allowance, which in the 1989-90 tax year was £5,000. In other words, you could make capital gains up to that amount without paying CGT.

Then there are certain gains which are not counted. The most common example is housing. If you sell your house you do not pay CGT on the profit you have made due to house price inflation. The same applies to your chattels, providing the proceeds do not exceed £3,000, as well as your car, pools winnings and Personal Equity Plans – which will be discussed in Chapter 13.

Up until the 1990-91 tax year married couples will be treated as one person as far as CGT is concerned – with one annual exemption – though transfers between the two do not count for CGT. This changes under independent taxation. From the 1990-91 tax year, each partner will have their own exemption limit, though transfers between the two will still be exempted.

Before having to pay CGT there is another issue which has to be resolved. You have to decide from what base you are counting the gain. There are two options. If the 'asset' was purchased or acquired after March 31, 1982 the initial purchase price plus expenses incurred, plus an allowance for inflation – as the inflationary growth factor is not taxable – will be the base figure for calculating the gain or loss.

But if the asset was held before March 31, 1982 you have the choice of opting for a different valuation. You can either use the original cost of the item or its market value at the time, or you can use the post-March 1982 method of calculating as outlined above.

If you do have to pay CGT then it is paid at income tax rates as if it were added to your income. This means that there are now two rates of CGT in 1989-90 tax year – 25 per cent and 40 per cent.

Obviously, the smart investor will choose whichever leads to less CGT being paid.

And what about inheritance tax?

I read recently that inheritance tax – known as IHT – was an extremely complicated tax. Well, it is to a certain degree, but the fundamental principles are straightforward enough.

If you die, and the total value of your estate in the 1989-90 tax year is worth more than £118,000, then you may be liable to IHT.

With the growth in house prices over the years, many people do not realize that the value of their 'estate' – which includes their investments – may mean that they are liable to IHT.

What you, the smart investor, therefore needs to know is how to avoid having your estate ravaged by the taxman after you die.

Firstly, estates up to £118,000 fall into the nil IHT rate band and so do not have to pay tax. And, husbands and wives should not be too concerned should one die, as the estate is passed on to the other partner without liability to IHT.

The best way to help avoid the taxman is to make lifetime gifts. However, IHT is structured so that you cannot give away your fortune just before you die in order to avoid the tax.

There are ways around the problem. You can make some gifts without liability to IHT. For example, you can give away up to £3,000 a year without liability to inheritance tax and then gifts of £250 on top, providing they are made to different persons.

You can also make exempt gifts of varying sizes to your

children, grandchildren, or even a friend if they are getting married. And you can also give gifts to charities or political parties.

But if you really want to shift large amounts of your estate to friends or relatives then you have to do it during your lifetime, and so you take the risk of having to pay tax.

It works like this. If you make a lifetime gift – say some property to a friend or relative – providing you do not die within seven years, then IHT would not be payable.

However, if you die within the seven years, then IHT would be payable at a higher or lower rate depending on whether your demise is soon after making the gift or say six years after.

There is a sliding scale which means that if you die within 0-3 years of making the gift IHT is liable to be paid on all the gift, while between 3-4 years just 80 per cent is liable. This tapers down so that in year 6-7 just 20 per cent of the value of the gift is liable. And when tax is paid, it is paid at a rate of 40 per cent.

Now you can see why IHT is thought to be a complicated tax. While the principles are straightforward enough, the rules surrounding it are complex and so you are best advised to seek further advice on the matter should you feel you may be liable.

Accountants dealing in personal taxation are probably the best people to see, whether on matters of income tax, capital gains tax or IHT. Some independent financial advisers and larger solicitors also have tax departments which might be able to help. For more about seeking further advice, see Chapter 5.

FOUR

Banking Your Cash

The current account revolution

Banks and building societies are as important to the investor as a knife and fork are to a gastronome.

Traditionally, they fulfil two primary functions – a place in which to park your cash, and a place in which to invest.

But now there have been two major developments which have brought these two functions closer together.

The development of interest-bearing current accounts now has a major bearing on where to park your money and the intense competition between financial institutions has a bearing on where to 'invest' your savings.

The Nationwide Anglia Building Society, closely followed by the one-time building society, the Abbey National, in my view should take credit for a major change in banking as we know it.

In May 1987 the then Nationwide Building Society, using new powers vested by the 1986 Building Society Act, became the first of its kind to launch an interest-bearing current account, known as FlexAccount.

The development, which had much earlier been flagged by a Co-operative Bank current account, was quickly followed by the Abbey National and it immediately put pressure on the big high street banks to offer competing products. They were slow to respond, and the two building societies quickly began to attract their own, and more importantly, new customers to their accounts.

What made the accounts so attractive was that for the first time, the dull old current account, which had previously been used only as a money transmission facility, suddenly became an investment in its own right.

After all, if you could actually make money on your current account, albeit a relatively small amount given the low interest rates offered, then the pressure was on you to change.

The prospect of the banks losing customers to the building societies was eventually met some 18 months later, when the first bank, Lloyds, responded by announcing that it too would provide an interest-bearing current account.

All this led to a flurry of activity, with every bank announcing a whole range of differing accounts to meet differing needs.

This 'consumerist'-driven reaction – to meet different needs – was in itself a revelation, because customers were perhaps for the first time being offered tailormade accounts to suit their needs.

Banks and some building societies were already offering higher interest cheque accounts – accounts which were similar to the basic current account, but demanded higher balances.

But the new developments made interest-bearing accounts more accessible to a wider audience.

Investing with your current account

Most people these days use current accounts both as a place to put their salary and for money transmission purposes, using cheques, debit cards and the now familiar hole-the-wall cash machines.

It stands to reason that you should make the best use of your money while it is parked in that account. But actually deciding which account to choose is something of a headache, and, certainly, the best account for you is the one which you think best suits your needs.

I can offer a few points which might help you choose an account. Firstly, you will generally find that the more interest offered on these accounts, the more it will cost you should you overdraw.

In fact, interest-bearing current accounts should not be used at all, if there is any question of your overdrawing regularly. Indeed, you could find that such accounts prove to be quite expensive if you are in the habit of going into the red.

Beware of those accounts which claim to be charge-free – you could find that you have to pay fees when the account is overdrawn by a relatively small amount. Check, too, the rates of interest charged should you go into the red, and also look to the differences in charging between authorized and un-authorized overdrafts.

The banks and building societies do not like you overdrawing without their say so – you could find that you are penalized pretty heavily if you do not ask their permission before going into the red.

Take note, also, of the higher interest cheque accounts which are similar to normal interest-bearing cheque accounts but require higher minimum balances for a higher rate of interest.

With such accounts you always need to keep an eye open to make sure that the high balance might not be better placed in a high-interest deposit account.

There is no real common denominator with these new current accounts – except that they pay interest. To get the best deal you really need to shop around – and that is not easy.

Tenacity, therefore, is just one of the secrets of successful investment.

Getting your cash from A to B

As I said, one of the primary reasons for a current account was to provide a place to park your cash. But there is more to current accounts than simply financial parking lots. The current account is one of the best aids to budgeting, and if used wisely can help make you money.

With interest-bearing current accounts you should try to keep as much of your money in your account for as long as possible.

This can be done easily enough through the budgeting process using standing order and direct debit payment systems. But make sure these facilities cost you nothing – and some accounts only allow a certain number of transactions before charging begins.

For example, if you do not have to pay your community charge bill in one go, then why not pay it in instalments – providing that is, the total bill is not going to cost more. By keeping your money in your account, you, rather than your local council, are earning interest.

The same process applies to most household bills, although you must be careful with your gas, electric, telephone and water rates, that your budget account with the relevant utility does not involve paying too much in advance.

The use of the cash dispenser is also a useful aid. By keeping cash in your account rather than in your wallet, you stand to get a better return on your balances. Going to a convenient cash till regularly is therefore better – and safer – than carrying a wad of notes around with you.

Cheques are still widely used, despite the plastic card revolution. Remember that using a cheque to pay bills delays the debiting of your account for around three working days, so leaving time to earn a bit more interest.

The new debit cards are extremely convenient as a payment method and should simply be regarded as paperless cheques – so they, too, are a useful way of delaying payment in order to maintain your balances.

All this monitoring of your money is made easier by the use of home banking – using your telephone to contact your bank electronically – though few institutions currently have such schemes. However, the merits of such systems must be measured against the albeit low charges and the time taken to talk to your bank electronically over your telephone.

Another development, led by Midland Bank, is the concept of direct banking – a centralized system where the bank has no branches: clients carry out all transactions by telephone. Midland's 'First Direct' was the first bank of this kind. They pay better rates of interest, so are worth considering.

But what about my savings?

The intense competition between the banks and building societies has meant two thing for the saver. Firstly, the range of accounts offered has multiplied so that anyone with an old bank or building society deposit account needs to ensure they now have the most 'suitable' product for their needs.

And secondly, as a result of the widening of the range of deposit accounts, there is greater vigilance needed in checking and double-checking the interest rates offered on your particular account to ensure that you are getting the best deal.

What the investor has to keep in mind is that deposit accounts follow certain basic principles as far as interest is concerned. Firstly, *the more you invest the more you get* and secondly, *the longer you invest, the more you get*.

All else stems from these two main rules. From your point of view, therefore, all you need to identify is what sort of deposit account suits your needs.

It is obvious that an investor with a relatively small amount of money who can afford to invest long-term could well choose a deposit account different from his neighbour who also wants to invest long-term but with a much larger amount of money.

Similarly, an individual with a large amount who wants to invest short-term, could well choose a different account from his neighbour who has a small amount of money but also wants to invest short-term.

So which account should I choose?

The banks and building societies have not made it easy for the investor to choose among types of deposit account. Frankly, it is not in their interest to do so. They would prefer you to come into their branch in the high street and let them provide you with an account from their range which best suits your requirements.

The problem with this approach is that the account offered may not suit all your requirements, and you may find that the bank next door is offering a better rate of interest.

You should read your newspaper at the weekends to check out just what different banks and building societies are offering their customers.

A strength and danger of your familiarity with a bank or building society is the natural temptation for you to stick with the same institution year in year out, simply because you always have done business with them.

That approach does not always work in your best interest, so beware of the 'lethargy effect' – the tendency by some people never to check what is going on around them in the savings and investments market.

So when we do go shopping around what will we find? One of the first things that you will note is the bewildering array of descriptions. On the deposit account side you will find 'Gold', 'Platinum' and 'Sterling' accounts, while interest-bearing current accounts will come as 'Orchards', 'Vectors' and 'Classics'.

What you really need to know is what type of account is being offered, and what they do for you.

What do the banks have to offer?

So let us start with the banks. Many of the accounts that come to your attention are ones which are probably familiar to you – the old 'notice' and 'seven day' accounts. With the former you have to give a specific level of notice before you can withdraw your money – perhaps one week, two weeks, a month, three months or more.

These are the bank's basic deposit account and are in direct competition with the building societies who often offer better rates of interest.

The seven day account – or simply the deposit account – is similar to the notice account, in that you have to give seven days' notice. However, in this case you can get your hands on your money straight away, but with the loss of seven days' interest.

Again, the seven day account has run up against the building societies, so you have to compare which is best for you.

In both cases, for reasons I mentioned in the previous chapter, these accounts are not very good for the non-taxpayer because tax is deducted from the interest at source and cannot be reclaimed.

Poor interest on such an account, allied with this fact, could be bad news for the non-taxpayer. A further problem is the accessibility of your money. Usually, you have to go into a branch and collect it – you cannot withdraw money from such accounts from a cash dispenser.

A more modern account is the cash card account. These are similar in operation to interest-bearing current accounts except they do not offer a cheque book, and so the interest rate is often higher. Cheques are expensive for the banks, so expect higher interest if the account does not have one.

The best-known cash card account was launched by the Halifax Building Society; however, even the nature of this is due to change with the advances in types of account. The TSB also offers such an account, and is attractive particularly to younger customers who prefer using 'new' rather than 'old' technology.

Again, these accounts are bad news for non-taxpayers, though good for the free payment of direct debits and standing orders, so they are a useful aid to budgeting.

The big investment vehicles with the banks are those where you save regularly, occasionally and rarely.

The savings account is a bread and butter account offering immediate access for minimal sums of money and is identical to those offered by building societies.

The big high street banks take more seriously the high interest deposit accounts. You can only open these accounts with a 'minimum sum' ranging from £500 to £2,000. In return you get an 'attractive' range of interest – though not always competitive – and you can also get immediate access to your money providing you are careful to maintain the minimum amount.

They are a good place for taxpayers to save, though again, the non-taxpayer would be better off elsewhere.

Finally, there is the deposit account for the long-term saver. Term accounts are the best payers in terms of interest but the most inflexible type of account from the point of view of access to your money.

Typically, you have to invest for periods of over a year – often up to five years. If you need to get your hands on your money you could pay heavily in loss of interest.

And what about the building societies?

The great rivals of the banks are the building societies – the great mutual institutions created to meet housing needs for the benefit of their members. That is, of course, how the building societies like to see themselves, though in reality the core of their business is still housing finance.

However, that is where the link with Victorian ideas of mutuality ends. The fact is that Britain's building societies are now highly competitive operations, with slick marketing machines, which strive to attract your money.

The end result is an array of different type of deposit – they prefer to call them 'investment' – accounts, designed for every type of saver.

Because the building societies concentrate on personal lending and borrowing, and because they do not have to pay dividends to shareholders, the rates of interest are often very keen when set against the banks, so you must shop around.

This has been particularly true since the building societies became free to tap funds from the money markets instead of having to rely on deposits from savers.

But, like the banks, the building societies still have hang-overs from the past and you can still open a 'share' account which offers poor rates of interest in return, when compared with the newer more 'tailored' accounts.

Take for example the cash card account – I mentioned the one from the Halifax earlier. Cardcash was the Society's first attempt to break the bank's dominance of the current account cheque market.

However, while these excellent accounts paid good rates of interest, they suffered from not being able to offer cheque books. Indeed, the Halifax Building Society sincerely believed that the plastic card would spell the end of cheques as a method of money transmission – they were wrong, and now offer a new account with a cheque book.

But, like all these deposit accounts, from the non-taxpaying investor's point of view, interest is taxed at source and cannot be reclaimed.

The building societies' basic savings account is the instant access account designed for those who want instant access to their cash. For those who can leave their money invested longer the notice account is better.

Most notice accounts offer a set rate of interest for a given level of notice – seven days, one month, and three months are usual. However, there is a new account now available which tailors the interest rate offered to the amount of notice you give the building society. This is an innovative approach and offers investors more flexibility – which is a good thing!

Another twist to the notice account is that which guarantees a set level of interest above the society's basic share rate. Such an account may offer, say, three per cent above the ordinary share rate – which might be, say, seven per cent – offering 10 per cent in all.

The building societies also offer accounts which are designed to generate monthly income from a lump sum investment and others which offer higher rates of interest in return for regular savings.

It is pretty difficult to sort the wheat from the chaff when selecting either bank or building society accounts because of the wide variety of product names used.

Building societies, for example, have used the term 'bond' in order to describe an account which is in reality a notice account. Such 'bonds' might, for example, call on you to leave your money on deposit for a one-year period in return for a guaranteed rate of interest.

So it is up to you as the investor to spot opportunities among the offerings from banks and building societies.

FIVE

Investing – How To Avoid Losing Your Shirt!

So you want to play safe?

The banks and building society deposit accounts are regarded by most people as being 'safe' investments.

After all, providing the bank or building society does not go bust – and there is more about this later – then your deposit is safe. Or is it?

Just how much can you rely on deposit accounts to fulfil the primary investment need of seeking a good return on your capital?

It stands to reason that if you take no risk by putting your money in a deposit account, then you cannot expect a great reward – and often you do not really get one! This is because of the effects of inflation which can whittle away at the interest provided by your deposit account.

For example, if inflation is standing at eight per cent and your building society is paying nine per cent net, then the growth in value of your money is just one per cent per year 'in real terms'.

The effect of inflation on deposit accounts over the years has been marked, and, indeed, there have been times when inflation actually overtook rates being paid on deposit accounts so that 'investments' were actually losing money in real terms.

If you look at figures supplied by the unit trust industry's trade association, the UTA, you find that an investment of £1,000 in a building society high rate deposit account would have risen to £1,520 over five years – a return of £520 on your original deposit.

However, by the time inflation is stripped out of this figure the 'real' return falls to just £227.

The position is similar if you look over the past ten years. Over ten years such a building society account with £1,000 invested would have risen to £2,388, a return of £1,388. But again, once inflation was stripped out, this would have fallen to £287.

But worse is yet to come. The high inflation of the 1970s hammered deposit accounts. If you look at the 15-year figure, £1,000 invested would have grown to £3,513. But when inflation is stripped out you get a negative return.

In fact, once inflation is stripped out of the 15-year figure the real value of your £1,000 investment would have fallen to just £703.

The fact is that inflation has to be taken into account when investing, and just as your status in the tax hierarchy dictates which sort of investments you should enter into, so does the presence of inflation.

While we in Britain invest quite heavily in stocks and shares, the same is not true in places like Germany where, in recent history, inflation has been very low.

The effect of low inflation has meant that this desire to constantly out-perform the nation's inflation rates has been less of a factor in the Federal Republic, and so a thriving bond market – a market in Government borrowing instruments – tends to dominate the investment scene.

Conversely, the fact that deposit accounts have not always kept ahead of inflation has meant that we in Britain have been prepared to take more risks, and so stock market-related investments have become important.

Yet, despite the inflation effect and the fact that deposits can be hit quite hard in periods of high inflation, deposits and certain other forms of low-risk investments will always thrive.

I said earlier that the type of investment you choose is governed by where you fall in the tax spectrum. Well, the type of investment you choose is also governed by how much money you have available to you.

Deposit accounts – regardless of the inflationary effect – are the right types of investment for those without high incomes and savings.

The very fact that Mrs Jones – a retired person living solely on the state pension with a small amount of savings – has invested in a building society, reflects a good decision on her part. She has tailored her investment according to her circumstances.

And so must you!

Setting out your objectives

Our Mrs Jones managed to balance her financial position against her objectives very well and came to the right decision – or did she? Do not forget building societies deduct tax at source and Mrs Jones cannot claim it back.

In fact, Mrs Jones did make the right decision, because Mrs Jones knows she is about to sell her big old house in favour of moving into sheltered accommodation, and she needs to be able to put her hands on her savings quickly over the next few months.

Mrs Jones is going to live with her old friend Miss Mills who is in similar financial circumstances but has invested her money with National Savings because, unlike Mrs Jones, she needs an income, but does not need quick access to her capital.

Our two new acquaintances have therefore worked out their needs and priorities – it might not be so easy for you to do the same.

Let us take an example to illustrate the point. Mr and Mrs Smith are both aged 30, have one child and another is on the way. They own their own house, but have a mortgage of £20,000. Mr Smith has been successful in his job and has worked for his company since he left school. He is now considering leaving to set up on his own. Mrs Smith is a teacher, and is thinking that in a few years' time she will go back to work. She earns a small amount of money at present from a part-time job.

The point is that the Smiths' circumstances are infinitely more complicated than those of our elderly friends, Mrs Jones and Miss Mills.

So how do they – and how do you – manage to cope with making a decision about your investments when you are not even sure what a particular investment has to offer?

The answer is to draw up a strategy, in much the same way as you had to draw up a budget for your money. Part of the strategy will be aimed at deciding what your objectives are and what risks are acceptable.

Once you have done that then you have to decide whether or not you need further advice. In the case of our elderly friends, the options are not great and so perhaps further advice, over and above knowing what each investment is and does, is probably unnecessary.

But what about the Smiths? Almost certainly, the Smiths will need further advice on planning their financial futures before making investment decisions to ensure they are aware of the risks involved.

The fact is that for the majority of private investors, like you, me and the Smiths, the biggest risk is making the investment in the first place.

How can we – the general public – make up our minds about an investment if we are unable to grasp precisely the basic questions concerning what an investment has to offer, why we need it, what it can do, and what other options are available?

Like it or lump it, there comes a point when all of us have to go out and seek further advice – a process that can be fraught with difficulty.

For example, who should you go to – your bank manager, building society manager, solicitor, insurance agent, accountant, or your psychiatrist, doctor or guru?

The fact is, when it comes to investments you enter a whole new ball game – and that 'ball game' is perhaps better known in the financial services industry as the Financial Service Act.

Investor protection and the Financial Services Act

One of the best ways of avoiding risk is to put your money into something that is regulated by the Government so that if a dodgy company or firm goes bust, you do not lose your shirt.

Britain always has had a degree of investor protection but by the mid 1980s the system was felt to be inadequate. The government decided to do something about it and and passed the Financial Services Act – the FSA – which provided a framework under which self-regulation could flourish.

This basically meant that those creating and selling financial products and services to the likes of you and me would make up a whole host of rules which had to fall into line with a specially constituted body called the Securities and Investments Board – the SIB – whose job it was to interpret the Act.

The end result is an incredibly complex network of rules and regulations by which the industry has to abide, and a system of investor protection which, while worthwhile, is costly and has ultimately to be paid for by those buying investment products – again, you and me.

Despite the cost, the FSA is vitally important to the investor's decision-making because it provides a certain level of cover against things going wrong.

It does not stop you making a fool of yourself by investing in silly investments or by making bad decisions, but it does protect you against those selling you the products going bust or being dishonest.

As the SIB says in one of its brochures:

All investment carries some degree of risk, whether relating to business or general economic conditions. The existence of SIB no more removes the need for investors to pay attention to where they place their money than the existence of the Highway Code removes the need to look before crossing the road.

So what happens if you do cross the road, and a juggernaut rolls over your foot?

The FSA does provide a system whereby if you have a complaint you can go to the appropriate body and try to get the matter resolved.

If you have a complaint you have to work on two different levels. The first level comes as a results of the FSA and consists of the company and its regulatory authority. In the first instance, you should always complain to the company which sold you the investment if a problem arises.

If you are not happy with the way that works out, then try the company's regulatory authority – known in the business as a Self-Regulatory Organization – the 'SRO'.

There are a number of SROs covering different issues. For example there is The Securities Association – the TSA (see page 128), which covers firms who sell and give advice on stocks and shares – primarily stockbrokers.

Then there is the Financial Intermediaries, Managers and Brokers Regulatory Organization – better known as FIMBRA (see page 127). This SRO deals primarily with insurance brokers who sell life assurance and unit trusts.

There is the Association of Futures Brokers and Dealers – the AFBD (see page 126) – whose firms consist of the futures and options dealers, while the Investment Management Regulatory Organization – IMRO (see page 127) covers those companies who manage unit trusts, investment trusts and pension funds.

Then there is the Life Assurance and Unit Trust Regulatory Organization – LAUTRO (see page 127), which covers the insurance companies and friendly societies.

Even other professionals, such as lawyers, accountants and actuaries, must be registered through their own professional body, which will be, not an SRO but a Recognized Professional Body – 'recognized' by the SIB.

All these SROs and RPBs are places where you can go should you need to complain about any problems with your investment over and above the normal risk-taking issues.

But there is a second level for you to take your complaints. And this level, apart from the SIB itself, falls outside the Financial Services Act.

The Ombudsman system is an informal system designed to resolve conflicts quickly. There are ombudsmen covering banking, insurance and unit trusts, and all provide an easy way of resolving a conflict with your bank, insurance or unit trust company.

But within the Financial Services Act, at the head of the regulatory system is the Securities and Investments Board. SIB has the power – as do the SROs – to stop a company trading if it feels there is a problem. In fact, you cannot sell investment products at all if you are not registered with an SRO or the SIB direct.

From the investor's point of view, one of the big plus points about the SIB is the Investor Compensation Scheme.

Under this scheme, if the investment firm in which you have put your money goes bust, then you could receive up to 100 per cent of your first £30,000 invested, and 90 per cent of the next £20,000. So if you had invested, say, £50,000, then you would get at least £48,000 back.

Again outside the scope of the FSA, the ombudsmen can also recommend awards to the investor – up to £100,000 – and the financial institutions usually abide by their recommendations.

In addition, there is more protection given under the Building Societies and Banking Acts, just in case one of those institutions goes under.

In the case of the building societies, up to 90 per cent of the investor's deposit is protected up to a maximum of £20,000, while under the banks' deposit protection fund, 75 per cent of the first £20,000 is protected. Insurance policies are also covered under the Policyholders' Protection Act so that policyholders will receive 90 per cent of the money owing to them.

Where to seek advice

If you need further advice on investments then it stands to reason that the people who sell investments are the people who give advice.

However, under the Financial Services Act, when it comes

to buying life assurance and unit trusts – both of which I delve into in later chapters – there are two different types of 'adviser'. There is the adviser who works for a company and sells only that company's investments, and another who sells the investment products of all companies.

This principle also applies to financial institutions who sell investments. For example, a building societies might sell the products of one life assurance company and so is said to be 'tied' to that company, or it may sell the products of all companies.

From the investor's point of view, the difference between the two types of adviser is important to grasp. Say you decide to invest in unit trusts. Naturally you might want to invest in one which has done very well in the past – perhaps you might want to invest in the best performer over the past three years?

What happens then if a 'tied agent' – the representative of one company – does not happen to have that particular unit trust. He cannot sell another company's products, and so you cannot get what you want from him.

So what do you do? You go to the person who can choose from the whole market. These independent advisers are better known as independent financial advisers (IFAs) – because they are independent of any company.

Similarly, you will remember the bit in Chapter 2 about some endowment policies growing at a much faster rate than others – then again these can be identified by IFAs so that if you want a top performing insurance company then you can be sure of getting one.

The difference between the company representative and the independent financial adviser should only really concern you when you buy life assurance and unit trusts.

But whatever type of adviser you go to, they must all satisfy two primary requirements under the Financial Services Act. Advisers must 'know their customer', which means being aware of your full circumstances before offering advice, then they must offer 'best advice', which means they must give the best advice available to them.

Most advisers are paid by commission or their wages are

topped up with a bonus system. What they must not do, therefore, is simply sell you a product which you do not need, so that they can get their commission – that is illegal under the FSA.

And they cannot sell you anything until they have fully probed your circumstances. This inevitably means a lot of form filling to get your details including your income, your highest rate of tax, pension arrangements, assets, investment income, personal health, loans, debts and overdrafts, other investments, existing life cover – in fact all the items which you need to take into account before deciding what investment to make.

The adviser must be fair in his criticism of a product, he must disclose its disadvantages, and perhaps most important of all, he must be truthful.

All advisers must be properly trained by a company registered with an SRO, RPB or the SIB.

So let us start investing; and let us start with our non-taxpaying elderly friends, Mrs Jones and Miss Mills.

SIX

National Savings

An ideal investment for the big and the small

Like bank and building society deposit accounts National Savings' products are very much linked to prevailing rates of interest.

But unlike mainstream bank and building society products they have the distinct advantage among the range of either offering interest 'tax-free' or 'gross'.

In doing so, not only do they provide an advantage to the non-taxpayer who is provided with interest gross, but they are also advantageous to the higher rate taxpayer who does not have to pay tax on them.

These advantages vary among the National Savings range, and what might be good for the non-taxpayer might not be good for the higher rate taxpayer.

And what about those of you in the middle – the basic rate taxpayer? Although there is no reason why basic rate tax-payers should not invest in National Savings, increased competition from the banks and building societies has meant that many National Savings products may be uncompetitive as far as they are concerned.

Having said that, certain National Savings products are de-signed to 'lock in' investors for a certain number of years, and so the basic rate taxpayer might feel like taking a long-term view and invest at a known rate – more about this later.

Interest rates are therefore central when investing in National Savings products – many of which are five-year in-vestments and so are only useful if you can afford to tie your money down for that length of time.

55

The only real way the private investor can take a view on the longer term performance of interest rates is by studying what is being said in the media, particularly by the Government.

Other than that, there is very little the investor can do to control risk, other than to spread money between investments which offer a known return and those which do not.

And you need to know how to compare what is being offered; the following section should help to do this in the context of one particular National Savings product.

Yearly Plan – guaranteed return in a fluctuating world

A typical example of the five year lock-in type product from National Savings is the 'Yearly Plan'.

This product is really only suitable for higher rate taxpayers who can save regularly, as the plan needs to be held for five years in order to achieve the guaranteed return. It is worthwhile to higher rate taxpayers only because the rate of interest paid is guaranteed, and is paid gross.

In order to assess the real value of the product the investor has to compare the gross return against other products. Before you do that – a brief description of the Yearly Plan. The scheme provides a guaranteed rate of interest in return for a commitment by the investor to save regularly and invest a fixed amount via 12 monthly payments. The interest is guaranteed only if 12 payments have been made and held for five years.

Now let us run through what the investor – a higher rate taxpayer – has to do before deciding whether to invest in a Yearly Plan.

Take the example of Mr Shepherd who wants to invest when the Yearly Plan is offering 7.5 per cent gross. At the time, higher rate taxpayers are paying 40 per cent tax.

Mr Shepherd has £20 a month to invest – £240 a year – and is considering whether to put his money into a Yearly Plan or the building society, which is currently offering nine per cent interest net – that is, nine per cent after basic rate tax has been deducted.

He knows if he invests £240 today in a lump sum he will receive £21.60 in interest.

However, he also knows that because he is a higher rate taxpayer he has to pay additional tax. In fact he has to pay tax at his highest rate – that is 40 per cent – on his 'grossed up' income.

So now Mr Shepherd has to calculate how much he will make after tax has been deducted from the building society investment and compare it with the return from the Yearly Plan.

First, he has to work out how much interest is paid by his building society in gross, rather than net, terms.

Bearing in mind that basic rate tax is deducted from the interest paid on building society accounts, Mr Shepherd does the calculation £240 divided by 0.75 to get £320 – which represents the gross return over a year from the building society paying nine per cent.

Now he has to deduct tax at the higher rate from the gross amount. Mr Shepherd knows that the extra tax paid is not 40 per cent – the higher rate – but the difference between basic and high rate – between 25 per cent and 40 per cent, that is 15 per cent.

He works out that 15 per cent of the gross return of £21.60 is £3.24. Mr Shepherd now knows that his £21.60 will be reduced by a further £3.24, making a real return of £18.36 – the amount he will have earned on his £240 invested.

But in order to compare this return with that from the Yearly Plan, Mr Shepherd also needs to know what £18.36 represents as an annual return on the £240 as a percentage. He does the calculation and finds out it represents 7.65 per cent.

Mr Shepherd can see that the Yearly Plan offers, at 7.5 per cent, marginally less than that, but he has to take two things into consideration.

Firstly, he knows that the return from the building society account would actually be a bit less because the £240 is not paid in a lump sum but monthly; and secondly; interest rates can have a major impact on his returns.

Mr Shepherd knows that while the Yearly Plan offers a guaranteed rate, the building society account does not.

For example, Mr Shepherd knows that if interest rates are likely to rise over the next five years, then his Yearly Plan investment will earn less than prevailing rates, and so he could lose out.

On the other hand, if interest rates fall, Mr Shepherd knows that his investment is locked in at 7.5 per cent, and he could do rather well.

Let us look at it from the building society point of view. If Mr Shepherd goes with the building society, he knows that if interest rates fall, his return on capital falls, but he can at least move his money elsewhere – possibly even into a Yearly Plan – though he has to take the chance that National Savings may not have reduced the guaranteed interest rate to new investors.

Conversely, if rates rise, then Mr Shepherd does better with his variable rate building society account than with his Yearly Plan.

Ordinary account – an account for the kids?

Higher rate taxpayers and children or those on low pay might benefit from opening a National Savings ordinary account because part of the income received is treated as being tax-free.

However, to qualify for a reasonable return you must have at least £500 deposited to qualify for the highest rate of interest paid. If the account drops below £500 your return could be halved.

The good news is that you do not have to pay any tax on the first £70 of interest. Indeed, husbands and wives can hold joint accounts ensuring that the first £140 is tax-free.

The ordinary account should therefore be a good investment for non-taxpayers and high rate taxpayers; however, you should compare it with returns paid to ordinary bank and building society deposit accounts.

58

Investment account – the children's choice

When it comes to longer term savings the non-taxpayer would probably be better off with a National Savings investment account.

The account pays interest gross, but it is taxable, therefore it is not of so much use to the higher rate and basic rate taxpayer. However, it is of use to non-taxpayers, be they children or those on low income.

You have to give one month's notice of a withdrawal – so the investment account is not so good for those of you who might need to get your hands on your money quickly.

Interest is credited once a year – usually on December 31 – and entered into your bank book when you next go into a post office.

It is a good account for the kids because children under seven years of age can have one, although they have to wait until this age before they can make a withdrawal on their own signature.

Savings certificates – fixed-interest or index-linked?

Savings certificates are of particular interest to higher rate taxpayers because the interest paid is tax-free – though the basic rate taxpayer might be tempted.

They should be considered as a long term investment if you are to get the best out of them.

As with all National Savings, the investor needs to have a view on interest rates before deciding to invest.

Certificates come in two forms – 'fixed-interest' and 'index-linked'.

Fixed-interest certificates, as their name implies, offer a fixed rate of interest if held for five years. After five years, the interest rate changes to a variable rate known as the 'General Extension Rate' – which usually offers a much lower rate of interest.

Every 'issue' of the certificates goes by a name – for example, at time of writing this, the '34th Issue' was for sale, offering 7.5 per cent compound over five years.

It had a minimum purchase level of £25 with a maximum holding of £1,000.

Again, if you feel that a 7.5 per cent guaranteed return over five years is likely to prove worthwhile to lock into, then fixed interest certificates are for you.

Index-linked certificates are completely different except that interest is tax-free and you have to keep them for five years.

And they are a particularly good investment for those concerned about sudden rises in the rate of inflation, because these certificates aim to take away the pain of sharp rises.

They could therefore be of interest to non-taxpayers, but only when the return is less than that available from other forms of investment such as the investment account.

At time of writing the '4th index-linked' issue was on offer for sale and was paying 4.04 per cent over the going rate of inflation.

That means it paid out at a rate level with the rate of inflation plus 4.04 per cent.

After five years, however, the 4.04 per cent is dropped and the certificates grow at the prevailing rate of inflation.

You can get your money back on both kinds of certificate though the interest paid will be much less than that if held over five years.

Income bonds – ideal for non-taxpayers

Income bonds are an ideal investment for those non-taxpayers who want additional income. That is why they are often used by elderly people who have savings but who want to supplement their income.

The interest is taxable, but is paid in full at source. You can buy up to £100,000 in lots of £1,000, though the minimum investment is £2,000.

The rate of interest on income bonds is variable and tends to move in line with general interest rates such as those offered by the banks and building societies.

If you need to get your hands on your capital you have to

give three months' notice and you will only get half the interest on any amount repaid in the first year.

For people asking how they should arrange their affairs if they were to buy income bonds, the answer is simple: you need to buy enough to bring your income up to the point where you begin to pay tax.

Say you could earn £800 a year before your total income uses up your particular tax allowance. At time of writing income bonds were paying 11.5 per cent, so you would have to invest £6,956 in order to get an £800 return.

The problem is you cannot invest this odd number in income bonds – they are sold in lots of £1,000, and in any case you probably would not want to push yourself right up against your threshold in case an interest rate rise might push your income above your allowance. An investment then of say £6,000 – paying a return of £690 – would be more appropriate.

Capital bonds – a capital idea?

Capital bonds are the latest product from National Savings and are worth buying if you do not pay tax but want a long-term savings medium.

Providing you hold the bonds for five years you get the full amount of interest guaranteed. Under the first series – Series A – the interest works out at 12 per cent per year.

For the taxpayer, the problem with capital bonds is that you have to pay your tax in advance of the five-year anniversary, which is not particularly satisfactory in a high-interest-rate environment, where the tax paid in advance could well be earning interest elsewhere.

The minimum holding of capital bonds if £100 – there is no maximum. You can get your money back subject to three months' notice though you won't get any interest in the first year.

Taking a gamble – Premium Bonds

Premium Bonds are the strangest 'investment' of all, because there is no guarantee of any return.

However, as with most 'investments' you have to weigh-up

the risks. The odds of winning in the Premium Bonds draws is 11,000 to one, so £1,000 invested should result in a one-in-eleven chance of winning each draw. As the draw takes place once a month the odds narrow considerably over the year. In fact, the chances are you should win once a year with average luck.

That is worth considering if you are a higher rate taxpayer seeking a return on your money. A £50 win once a year represents a five per cent return tax free on your £1,000 invested. The return changes considerably if you win a £100, £500, £1,000, £5,000, £10,000 or £250,000 monthly prize.

In addition there are weekly prizes of £25,000, £50,000 and £100,000.

Of course, you cannot guarantee winning a Premium Bond prize and so you cannot guarantee a reasonable return. From a pure investment point of view they are not very good, and should only be used once other investment options have been exhausted.

Having said that, there is a great entertainment value in Premium Bonds, and I know that many people are prepared to forsake a reasonable return simply to receive the unexpected prize through the post.

National Savings's products can be bought through your local Post Office, which is where you should go if you need further advice. National Savings produces a large amount of useful literature, most of which is on display at local post offices.

For the non-taxpayer, National Savings produces 'A Guide To Savings For Non-Taxpayers', a useful document which provides non-taxpayers with a guide around the National Savings scene (see page 128 for address).

SEVEN

Life Assurance

Investment or protection?

As with many savings and investments, life assurance is worthwhile because it benefits from favourable tax treatment.

It is also a relatively cheap and efficient way to meet your financial needs, perhaps through savings plans or protection for your entire family. It can help fund your retirement or buy your house. In short, as an investment life assurance can cater for most needs.

There are two principle aspects of life assurance – protection and investment.

If you are married and perhaps have children then it is essential that you look to the first aspect of life assurance to provide adequate protection to cover your life, health, wages or house. All this should be done before taking the plunge into pure investment.

You should first seek protection through 'term' or 'temporary' life assurance or through 'whole of life' assurance. Term assurance provides cover for a specific length of time and hence is usually cheaper and attractive for younger people, while whole of life assurance provides more comprehensive cover and is therefore more expensive, but is particularly attractive to older people.

There are two principle types of investment within the insurance industry – endowment policies and annuities.

We have already come across endowment policies in Chapter 2, when we talked about endowment mortgages.

While term assurance is designed only to protect your life, an endowment policy also provides a vehicle to invest. Traditionally, endowments only provide a token amount of life cover and so they should be regarded only as savings and investments vehicles rather than vehicles which offer full life protection.

The attraction of endowments to you the investor is that they attract a lump sum 'payout' which will cover the mortgage should you die before the end of the term.

This is why endowments are used in conjunction with mortgages. The homeloan is taken out with a lender who charges you only for the interest. An endowment is also taken out, and grows over a number of years. At the end of the prescribed period – usually 25 years – the policy matures and hopefully enough tax-free money has accrued to pay off your mortgage. This is usually the case, and a surplus often arises which can be spent on whatever you wish.

The second type of investment is the annuity. This is a topsy turvey kind of insurance because instead of paying out on maturity or on your death – such as is the case with an endowment – the annuity pays an income to you in return for a lump sum investment.

It is a topsy turvey kind of assurance because its investment value depends on whether you can live longer than the insurance company expects you to do.

It stands to reason therefore that an annuity granted to a 70- year-old man will produce a greater income than one granted to a 70-year-old women, simply because women are expected to live longer.

Pensions are annuities in the sense that they are annuities deferred until retirement. In fact, as we shall see in the next chapter, pensions can be constructed in a number of ways using life assurance. For example, you could use an endowment to save for your retirement, and then use the lump sum to purchase an annuity to provide an income in retirement.

With-profits and unit-linked

The performances of insurance savings and investment policies all rely on the underlying investment of the pooled funds from the policyholders.

If you were to look back in history to the dawn of life assurance, you would find lives were protected by pooling small sums of regularly paid premiums, so that when someone died, their family could be given a sum of money.

It quickly came to be appreciated that not everyone died at the same time so the life fund had to be big enough to cope with all eventualities and demands upon it.

That meant that life companies began to accrue large sums of money which were invested and profits made on those investments. Such profits were in reality the profits of the members and so, once the company was satisfied that it could meet its responsibilities, the profits were shared out as and when they arose. Such profits were shared out as bonuses, and the 'with-profits' business was born.

With-profits policies guarantee that a minimum sum will be paid by the life company at the end of an agreed period. During that time, profits from invested funds can be shared among the policy holders in the form of bonuses.

These bonuses take a number of forms according to which company you invest with. However, for our purposes there are two main types of bonus – the 'reversionary' and the 'terminal' bonus.

Reversionary bonuses are those paid during the life of the policy – usually once a year. These days, life companies compete in the investment field to see who pays out the best reversionary bonuses each year.

The terminal bonus, on the other hand, is paid when the policy matures and, again, there is an element of competition among the companies.

However, as an investor you should be aware that some companies prefer to pay higher levels of reversionary bonus while others prefer to concentrate on the terminal bonus. For most purposes however, it is the total return which is considered to be important.

Remember, the declaration of a bonus is not guaranteed – only the minimum sum is guaranteed. Having said that, once the bonuses are declared they cannot be taken back.

No-one can predict what these bonuses are definitely going

to be so it is difficult for you the investor to choose between one company or another.

Some guidance can be sought from the past performance of companies, though this is no guarantee to the future. Having said that, as far as with-profits endowments are concerned, the same big names keep cropping up from year to year in the top ten performance league table. Past performance has therefore proved to be something of a guide to consistency.

But the with-profits method of investment is not the only form within the insurance industry. In more recent times, the industry has supplemented the with-profits approach with the 'unit-linked' method of investment.

Unit-linking is a relatively straightforward method of investing from the insurance companies' point of view.

The company creates a number of 'funds' which each has a specific objective which can either be a very general one – perhaps to achieve capital growth by investing through stocks and shares in international markets – or it might be a very specific one – perhaps to invest in the UK Gilts market. Unit-linked policies can be linked to property funds, equity funds or unit trusts.

Such a range of funds provides you with flexibility to switch between them – sometimes at a cost – so providing a choice of risk.

You therefore have to make the decisions at the outset in order to tailor the 'risk' aspect of the investment with the 'reward'.

If you can vary the risk, then unit-linked insurance policies are inherently more risky or safer than with-profits policies. However, given that you have the choice to tinker with the make-up of your unit-linked funds – the 'portfolio' in which you are invested – then effective measures can be taken to reduce risk, either at the outset, or perhaps in later years when you are less prepared to risk your money.

Unit-linked investments are, therefore, of less use where certainty is needed, though they can be managed to achieve certain objectives.

However, there is no guarantee with a unit-linked policy

that when you need the money, the underlying investments might not have dipped in value.

The secret of unit-linking is timing and planning. If your investment timing is right then you stand to do very well – better than with a with-profits policy whose performance is restrained by the need to cover the demands on the life fund.

And planning is important. By structuring your unit-linked policy to invest in more risky investments in the early years, and then safer funds in later years, you match your return to the level of risk you are prepared to accept at a particular time. Ironically, some insurance companies offer with-profits funds into which you can shift your investment later in its life in order to achieve that degree of safety.

Why invest in life assurance?

At the outset I said that one of the advantages of investing in life assurance in the first place is the tax advantages offered by endowment and annuity contracts.

Up until March 1984 endowment policies attracted Life Assurance Premium Relief – a tax relief on the premiums that you paid to the insurance company. The relief made pre-March 1984 policies very tax efficient, and anyone who still holds one would be well advised to hang on to it.

The other great advantage of the endowment, and the one which is most often pushed by the insurance salesman, is that the fund you build up is not subject to any taxation when it reaches maturity.

This tax-free status applies in most cases to the policy should you wish to get your hands on your money before the policy matures, though you have to be extremely careful in cashing in your policy – 'surrendering' it – before the maturity date because you are usually heavily penalized for doing so.

You should take note of these penalties because they add an additional element of risk. You have to ask yourself, 'Can I really afford to invest for 10, 15 or 25 years?'

One danger is this: if you surrender your endowment within ten years of taking out the policy, or before the expiry of three-quarters of the term if that is less than ten years, then any profits will be taxable if they push you into the higher rate tax band.

Despite the fact that there is a tax relief called 'Top Slicing' which takes into account the number of years over which the profit is earned, additional tax will reduce the return on your investment if surrendered early.

All this happens because endowments are 'qualifying policies'. Providing they stick to the rules then the policy 'qualifies' for tax relief.

Qualifying policies are those where contributions are paid at regular intervals, usually monthly, quarterly, half yearly or annually. The premiums also have to be spread evenly – no wonder therefore such policies are likened to savings plans.

But there are also policies which are 'non-qualifying' and they too have their own set of rules.

Non-qualifying policies are lump-sum policies where a single 'premium' is paid. A single lump of money is paid to the insurance company to buy such a policy – usually known as a 'bond'.

As with the endowment, the non-qualifying investment bond is, on maturity, tax-free at the basic rate of tax – but, unlike the endowment, the privilege for non-qualifying policies does not extend to the higher rate of tax.

The rules say that you can withdraw up to five per cent of the initial investment in each policy year without being taxed. This five per cent is a cumulative figure so if you do not use it the benefit mounts up over the years to maturity.

If you take out more than your five per cent entitlement then you will have to pay extra tax but only if your total income exceeds the basic rate band.

The same applies when the bond matures. Providing your income does not exceed the basic rate band, then you have little to worry about. Thankfully, Top Slicing also applies to bonds and so your tax liability, if any, is reduced.

The bad news is that if you are a basic rate taxpayer the only time you have to worry about bonds is when you are old enough to claim age allowance. This is because the income from the bond still counts as part of your total income when claiming age allowance.

The good news is that this applies only when you withdraw more than five per cent of your initial investment from the bond. Therefore the bond can be very effective – particularly as you can store up allowances from previous years, which makes good financial planning.

Nowadays, bonds tend either to be used by financial advisers as part of a comprehensive financial planning service to their clients, or to those who simply want to lock in at a particular rate of interest. Because they are a fairly complex instrument to monitor – in taxation terms – they are often ignored in favour of some other form of investment, such as savings certificates.

You can overcome these difficulties by seeking independent financial advice. A good financial adviser should help you plan your finances with the successful use of bonds.

But what about annuities?

Annuities pay a regular income in return for a lump sum. In this sense they are a very simple assurance contract.

But, unlike normal life assurance, your estate cannot recover your money back once you die – unless you take insurance out to cover that eventuality, a process which is becoming more common these days. The risk element of an annuity, therefore, is firstly in deciding how much you can risk in order to provide yourself with additional income.

This question might not matter too much if you do not want to leave your money to an heir, but if you do, careful consideration has to be made of the value to you of the annuity.

The second level of risk comes in deciding how much you are prepared to commit to the annuity, knowing that you cannot get your money back once the contract has been entered into.

However, there are now many types of annuity to suit most investors' needs. As with endowment policies, you have to shop around to get the best deal, and, as with bonds, you should seek advice from an independent financial adviser.

For example, you can tailor your annuity to ensure that it is taken out on joint lives so that if you die then your partner will continue to reap the benefit of the plan.

An area where this is obviously useful is when an annuity is taken out with a home income plan whereby equity is released from the value of your home in order to buy an income via an annuity.

The tax advantages of an annuity come with the way the income is paid to the policyholder. The payment is considered to be split into two parts – part repayment of capital and the rest income.

The capital element is tax-free while the income element is treated as ordinary investment subject to income tax at basic and higher rates. The ratio between the two elements varies according to actuarial mortality tables – the older the policyholder the higher the capital content.

For example, at the age of 65 a man would receive around £72 in capital while a woman would receive £59. By the time they reach 80 the capital rises to £164 for men and £128 for women.

Some annuities offer guarantees, say for five, ten or 15 years. Under this scheme if you die, say, a year after taking out the annuity, it continues to be paid for five, ten or 15 years. The basic annuity is guaranteed for the life of the purchaser or the guaranteed period, whichever is the longer.

EIGHT

Pensions

One of the better investments?

Pensions are one of the best investments you can make because the tax advantages are so good. Like life assurance they afford protection in employment and, like annuities, they provide an income.

Unfortunately, pensions have got something of a reputation of being a bit of a dull subject, when from an investment point of view they certainly are not.

The fact is that pensions are one of the most important investments that you have to make, and so you need to grasp the basics in order to seize the opportunities open to you if you want to boost your return.

The problem for the investor is, however, that because pensions are such a long-term investment and because they are beset by rules and regulations, it is very difficult to assess which type of pension is the 'best' investment.

I said that pensions were like life assurance in that they offered protection in employment. So they do, but they also afford protection in another sense – in ensuring that your life-style is not devastated by the onset of retirement.

Saving for retirement is nothing new – indeed, pensions are not new – but the changes which have recently been wrought in the pensions industry amount to nothing short of a revolution.

Because these changes were aimed at providing greater choice, then it is incumbent on you the investor to start looking at what is best for your needs.

Let us start with the basics so you can understand the range of pensions opportunities open to you.

Firstly, there is the state pension – with exclusive membership to those in employment. Payment into the scheme is compulsory and made through your National Insurance contributions.

You might also have decided or – more to the point – your company may have decided to opt in or out of the State Earnings Related Pensions Scheme, otherwise known as SERPS.

This is a top-up scheme which boosts the state pensions of those who are 'contracted-in' to the scheme. Again, membership of SERPS comes through the payment of additional National Insurance contributions.

Unfortunately, the state pension, even when boosted by SERPS, is not very big. In the 1988-89 tax year the figure for the basic state pension for a single person who was not in SERPS was £41.15 – roughly one fifth of the average wage.

And, of course, you can only actually receive the pension when you retire – at the age of 60 for women and 65 for men. There is no early retirement provision in this scheme.

Clearly then, for most of us who have been in full employment during our working lives the state pension is not adequate to maintain us in the luxury to which we may have become accustomed!

So you have to top-up on your state pension in order to help make-up the shortfall between the state pension and your salary at retirement.

So what are the choices?

Your first big decision as an investor is to choose between the two principle types of pension on offer – a company pension and a personal pension.

As the name suggests the company pension is the one which is offered as a 'perk' by your employer – that is why they are often called occupational pensions.

These pensions are generally funded by your employer, though with most schemes you are expected to chip in your share if you want to become a member of the scheme. Not all schemes require you to make a contribution, and are therefore known as 'non-contributory schemes'.

Where you do have to put money into the scheme, then usually you are called upon to put in a percentage of your salary – say five per cent.

If you do not want to join the company scheme, but still want to start investing in a pension then you could opt for a 'personal' pension, in which case you make a private arrangement by setting up a scheme, usually with an insurance company, and you pay in much the same way as you would pay into an endowment policy, though with greater effect.

Whether you choose the company route or the personal pension route, the decision depends heavily on your personal circumstances. In many cases, the company pension is the best answer, while for others, the personal route is better.

The pros and cons of the company scheme

Not every company offers a pensions scheme, but those that do, offer one of two kinds.

Firstly, there is the 'final salary' type which is a pension linked directly to what you were earning in the run-up to retirement and the number of years you worked for the company.

This type of investment is not unlike a savings plan whereby you fund your own personal investment fund, in the same way as a unit-linked savings plan.

Such schemes, therefore, are in many respects a reward for loyalty, given that the pension is heavily funded by the employer – though the employee's contribution may be considerable.

Given this state of affairs, the pools of money which grow within a pension scheme over the years can become very substantial indeed, and while the investment returns might benefit the pension scheme, they rarely confer additional benefits to you the employee – it is only when you retire that you get additional benefits from good performance.

For the employee considering entering the company pension scheme the level of your pension at retirement is not determined by the return on the fund, as is the case with, say, an endowment policy; rather, the fund has simply to be big enough to meet defined objectives, which are laid out in a set of rules.

These rules will determine how much pension you will get for each complete year of employment with the company. The pension is worked out by comparing the number of years worked for the company against a chosen base. Often the base is fixed at 60 so that if you retire after, say, 30 years with the company then you get 30/60ths of the full pension which is related to your final salary. More generous pension funds might offer more generous terms, say 30/45ths or less generous ones 30/80ths.

But at the end of the day it is the years of service and final salary that really count. This can be a complex piece of arithmetic because the scheme rules might, for example, leave out bonuses and commissions which traditionally have boosted your income, and some might even take out a figure representing the state pension before making the calculation.

This is not the case with all company pensions schemes. On the contrary, there are those which do not rely on the final salary at all and are more akin to endowment policies.

These types of pension are known as 'money purchase' schemes and, like final salary schemes, are funded by the employer and employee. Because they are very simple to run, money purchase schemes are often the choice of small companies.

In this case the amount of pension payable at the end of your working life is determined not by fractions and final salary but by the amount you put into the scheme. When you retire this money funds an annuity, which provides an income in retirement.

With both money purchase and final salary schemes, you can take tax-free lumps sums – providing they fall within Inland Revenue rules – according to the size of your investment.

Why invest the company way?

The overriding reason for choosing a company pension is that as a long-term investment it promises the best deal you are likely to get – providing, that is, you stay with one employer for a large part of your working life and that you leave the company on a good salary.

These days the chances of that happening are somewhat remote, and indeed the overriding advantages mentioned above have to be toned down somewhat. After all, how many people these days are likely to stay with the same employer for the whole of their working lives?

So why then should you consider a company pension?

Despite the possibility of your not staying with the same employer, the structure of company pensions does offer a certain degree of security.

Firstly, you know that your investment is boosted by your employer's contribution so, in effect, you are buying certain benefits at a cheap rate.

What happens is that for a given percentage of your salary spent on your pension, you will get back a defined benefit linked to both the size of your final pre-retirement salary and to the number of years you have worked with the company.

You might not know exactly what your final salary might be in, say, 25 years time but at least you know that your pension will be commensurate to your salary and service, and that makes planning easier.

Then there is the question of the treatment of your pension on retirement. With a company pension you can either take a full pension – once the figures have been worked out – or you can take up to one and a half times your final salary in a lump sum and a reduced pension. Do not forget, your pension is counted as income and is therefore taxable.

But there is more to company pensions than just the cash, and these do apply to employees both before and after you retire. Death benefits come in the shape of lump sums and incomes paid to widows while in employment and after retirement – this is a perk which has to be evaluated in conjunction with the cost of life assurance.

It does appear, then, that individual circumstances do have a bearing on whether or not you go into a company scheme. If, for example, you are likely to move jobs, then you have to consider how 'portable' your pension is.

Some industries have schemes which make it easier for individuals to move around though generally 'moving equals losing' as far as company pensions are concerned.

Those people who feel they are likely to move a number of times in their working careers would, therefore, not be suited to company pensions schemes.

Personal pensions – a viable alternative

'Personal Pensions' have, in one sense, been around for a long time.

Self-employed people had long used what were known as Section 226 contracts in order to provide a way of investing for their retirement. Quite simply, these contracts enabled the self-employed to put by some money each month and receive tax relief on the premiums.

Over the years, the pot of money built up without being taxed for income or capital gain and on retirement the investor could use the money to buy an annuity in order to provide an income in old age.

These contracts still exist, but you can no longer buy them. Instead, the Government introduced a new kind of personal pension which acts in much the same way as the old 226 plans.

It was these new 'personal pensions' which sparked the revolution within the industry.

The main difference between the old and the new is not in the way they worked, but rather in the benefits they offered on retirement.

A personal pension allows you to take as big a pension as you like, though, as there is a cap on the level of contributions linked to your wages, then this figure is held down. If you are under 35 years old you can put in up to 17.5 per cent of your salary into a personal pension plan (or PPP). This rises to 20 per cent up to age 45, 25 per cent to age 50, 30 per cent to age 55, and 35 per cent to age 56 and over. You can take out as many PPPs as you like providing you keep within these limits.

On retirement you can take a tax-free cash sum of 25 per cent of your fund, though you should remember your actual pension will be taxed as income.

SERPS was revolutionized too

The Government not only decided to introduce these new pension plans in their general desire to make pensions more flexible. They also decided effectively to 'privatize' their own SERPS state pension top-up scheme.

Quite simply, those employees – and you might be one of them – who were paying the additional National Insurance contribution because their company was contracted into SERPS now had the choice of 'contracting' back out again and making their own personal arrangements. These arrangements of course, were to invest the money saved in personal pensions.

The Government decided to offer an incentive from the Department of Social Security to encourage people to move out of SERPS – because the scheme was getting a bit expensive – and also enabled them to transfer the money, including the employer's bit of the National Insurance contribution, into a PPP.

So should you 'opt out' of SERPS? The answer is 'yes' if you are young and 'no' if you are old. That is not very helpful to those of you aged around 40, who fall in the middle. However, the fact is that no-one really knows what is the turning point.

The actuaries have calculated that men under 45 and women under 40 should 'contract out'. You should seek advice on this matter, though, because that point is not fixed forever.

Boosting your pension – more changes

If you are in an occupational pension scheme then you might feel that you want to boost your pension so that you have greater benefits on retirement.

You can do this through additional voluntary contributions, otherwise known as AVCs.

Just as the personal pensions have limits on contributions so do company schemes, and this becomes important when you want to buy AVCs.

You can put up to 15 per cent of your salary into an occupational pension so you need to work out how much you are putting in at present and how much this would leave once deducted from 15 per cent of your salary.

As AVC contributions are invested in a separate account, you are effectively adding to a pool of your own funds. The AVC is not part of the main pension fund. In this way it is not very different from a personal pension plan so it was not surprising perhaps that the Government also decided to allow individuals to make their own AVC arrangements outside the influence of their companies.

With these new 'free standing' AVCs you still have to stick to the same rules as with the company AVCs – so why buy them?

The free standing AVCs offer you choice – the choice of who will invest your money for you. Therefore, you may feel that you will do a better job of choosing your own investment managers than your company.

Not all AVCs are structured in this way. In public service, pensions are boosted when you buy 'added years'. The concept is simple enough – you effectively extend the number of years that you have been employed by your current employer for pension purposes by paying additional contributions to your pension.

What happens if I retire early or change jobs?

As far as occupational schemes are concerned the benefits that you get on early retirement depend very much on your particular scheme's rules – some will be far more generous than others. You really have to consult your personnel department to check on the rules.

With PPPs the position is more straightforward. You can retire between the ages of 50 and 75 with a normal PPP, but only at the normal state retirement age if you have opted out and bought a SERPS PPP.

Changing jobs is another matter. For occupational pensions the choices are complex. There are three main options –

to leave your pension with your old company where the benefits will slowly grow in value, or, if your employer allows, your pension rights are 'valued' and then transferred to another scheme. Or you can cash in your pension, using the monies to buy a pension plan which is similar to a PPP.

Again, it is extremely difficult to know which path to take if you are changing jobs. However, it would be fair to say, that the third option – the 'Buy Out' approach – has proved popular in recent years, primarily because as with free standing AVCs, you get a choice of who will best manage your money. Good stock market returns for the insurance companies in recent years have meant better pensions for those taking this option.

Pensions – seek advice!

Pensions are very valuable investments in our financial planning arsenal. But, as you have no doubt gathered, they are very complex types of investment so you need to treat them with respect and seek further advice before joining a scheme.

And for those of you already in a scheme, you should review your position – perhaps you should be investing in an AVC? Or, you could even consider using your pension to buy your home through a 'pension mortgage'.

The personnel departments of larger companies can usually run through their particular pension scheme with you. Such schemes often use the services of actuaries, who can also help answer your questions.

On the personal pension side, as these are offered primarily by insurance companies, then you should turn to an independent financial adviser, in just the same way as you might if you want to buy a good endowment. Again, past performance is no guarantee of future performance, but at least an IFA will be able to identify a good company whose product best suits your needs. In addition, an IFA should be able to ensure that your pension 'fits' neatly alongside your other investments.

NINE

The Stock Market

A different sort of risk!

This chapter marks something of a watershed, in that until now the concept of 'risk' has been used to relate primarily to the dangers posed by inflation on interest-generating investments such as your deposit account.

But we also touched 'risk' when we looked in general terms at life assurance, particularly when comparing unit-linked and with-profits policies.

Then there was the 'risk' of simply not choosing the right insurance policy, whether an endowment or a personal pension plan. Here I advised that you contact an IFA for help in choosing the right investment.

Generally speaking, the above types of investment pose little threat – with the exception of unit-linked plans – to your 'capital'. Whatever happens with inflation, you know that the amount of money in your building society will not be reduced in amount whatever happens to interest rates – only the value of your money will be affected.

For many people, the risk of high inflation is unacceptable and many decide to take greater risks in order to protect their investments.

The stock market has proved to be the place to go simply because here you are in line, not only to generate an income from your investments, but to get capital growth as well.

In order to achieve these objectives you have to take even greater risks – and there are very few stock market investments which have proved to be absolutely safe, no matter what the experts say.

The secret of successful stock market investment is the

management of risk. You have to tailor your cloth to suit needs - you simply cannot take unacceptable risks.

Just as important, you should not enter the stock market in the belief that you can make a quick buck! You must aim to provide a return which balances risk and reward – a return which proves better than a savings account, but one which does not expose your capital to great threat.

Remember the gardener at the beginning of the book? Don't plant your crops on the open hillside – grow them under glass! It might be more expensive, but you are more certain of a successful future.

Are we ready to invest?

Before we start looking at the markets let us make sure we have managed to sort out our personal finances, by going through the following questions:

- Have you made your mortgage arrangements? Are you fully aware of what can happen if interest rates move up?
- Have you checked your tax position and your overall income from wages and investments?
- Have you put aside some 'emergency' money in your current and deposit accounts to cover both expected and unexpected expenditure?
- Have you checked to ensure that you are aware of the protection afforded to investors by the Financial Services Act? Do you know the difference between a company representative and an independent financial adviser?
- Have you looked at National Savings in the context of your tax position to see if this is a useful place to invest longer term?
- Have you sorted out your general insurance to cover the car, house, contents, etc?
- Have you life assurance to ensure the family is okay if you are taken ill or worse? Are your family, health, mortgage, and salary covered for every eventuality?
- Have you sorted out your pension arrangements?
- Do you have any money left to invest?

If you have done all that and the answer to the last question is 'yes' then we can start looking at some more risky investments.

What do I want from my investment? – the case for gilts

Given that you hope to achieve both an income and capital growth from your investment it stands to reason that your investment can be either orientated to achieve more growth, or it can be directed to achieve more income.

One of the most popular forms of income-generating investment has been Government securities. These securities are better known as 'gilts' because the document of ownership once used to be edged with gold.

The Government issues gilts in order to raise cash – a function which in recent years has been supplemented by the privatization of state assets and the reduced need to raise public monies because public spending has fallen so dramatically.

So, when you invest in gilts you are actually giving the Government money and your reward is a given rate of interest, usually paid half-yearly by cheque.

They work like this. The Government issues the gilts, and you might buy £100 worth. In return you get a rate of interest – known as the 'coupon' – which, in order to illustrate the argument, we will say is eight per cent. That rate will be guaranteed until the gilt matures – in our example, say in 1999. In 1999, you then get your £100 back.

In many respects, therefore, gilts are a very simple investment and not unlike National Savings capital bonds, the first issue of which is offering 12 per cent guaranteed over a five-year period.

However, gilts are a bit different from capital bonds because gilts can be bought and sold in the stock market 'before' they mature. Now this is a very important point – and herein lies the secret to what makes gilts a risky investment.

You must ask yourself, 'What is this gilt worth to me?' In our example, the gilt cost £100 – this is said to be its 'nominal' value. But it also has a 'market' value, which on the day it was bought was £100.

However, because our eight per cent gilt can be resold in the market its price can rise and fall. And, if you have not already guessed, it is the rise and fall of interest rates which are the driving force behind gilts.

Say we bought our eight per cent gilt on a day when your building society was paying seven per cent. Obviously, the gilt at eight per cent was the better investment because it was generating a higher rate of interest – a higher return – from the same amount of capital invested.

If, a week later, the building society interest rate had dropped from seven to five per cent, then your gilt was even more valuable because it continued to pay eight per cent. So if you wanted to sell your gilt you know that it is worth more to you and others now than when you bought it. Therefore, instead of your gilt's market value being £100 it might now be worth £101.

If you sold it, you not only would have gained an 'income' from your investment of eight per cent, but your 'capital' would have grown by £1.

That is all well and good. But what happens if interest rates rise and instead of your building society offering seven per cent, it offers 10 per cent? Clearly then the building society offers a better return than your gilt. If you want to sell, then you could well find that its value has fallen to £99 in the open market – and you would have made a loss.

If you are considering buying gilts you should be prepared to keep a close watch on interest rates, buying when you think interest rates might go down and selling when you think interest rates are going up.

So what are the implications of this for the investor? Well it is quite straightforward. If you invest in gilts because you want to supplement your income, say in retirement, then you must accept that your capital could be eroded if interest rates rise above the fixed interest rate offered by the gilt, or indeed, the opposite could happen.

There are other influences on the market value of gilts. For example, you know that on the redemption date the government will pay back the £100. So the closer you get to that redemption date, the closer the market value of the gilt you hold moves back to £100. After all, no-one will pay £102 for the gilt one day knowing that it is only going to be worth £100 the next!

Gilts come in all shapes and sizes with varying 'coupons' and values. Some will be dated gilts, but be aware that some others will be undated.

There are also 'index-linked' gilts where the coupon and the nominal value of the gilt is linked to the rate of inflation.

You can buy new issues of gilts through your daily newspaper, though most selling is done in second-hand gilts, which can be bought and sold on the Stock Exchange.

Seek advice on the matter from your bank manager, financial adviser or stockbroker if you are interested.

You can also buy gilts at your Post Office through the National Savings Stock Register. This has a distinct advantage because the income from the investment is paid gross, rather than net which is the case if you buy from other sources.

So should you buy gilts? Gilts are a good investment if you need an income because you know the income is guaranteed, as is your capital – provided you are able to leave it until it matures.

They are also a flexible investment in the sense that you can tailor them to your needs. For example, you could go for high-yielding gilts – those which pay a high coupon – or low-yielding, which provide more of an opportunity for capital growth.

Because you do not have to pay capital gains tax on gilts, low coupon gilts are ideal for higher rate taxpayers as the main benefit is derived from the capital gain rather than income.

The non-taxpayer can also benefit from gilts, because the half-yearly income is paid gross through the National Savings Stock Register or can be reclaimed if you bought elsewhere.

Remember though, whenever you buy or sell gilts, and wherever you do so, you have to pay a commission on the purchase and on the sale.

Let's buy shares – the case for collective investments

With the moves towards wider share ownership, we have seen a massive upswing in interest in buying shares – often called 'equities'.

But the process of selling-off state assets, and the continual round of privatization 'issues' has had the unfortunate effect of making some people lose sight of their investment strategy.

Instead of carefully planning the purchase of shares as part of a wider investment strategy, we have simply dipped into the privatization pot and taken our share – often with good result for ourselves.

But you have to realise that buying shares outside the privatization area is quite a different matter. For example, you do not get the best value when buying shares unless you buy in large amounts – perhaps £3,000–£5,000 worth. Now that is a large sum to spend, and on quite a different scale to the privatization issues where you could pick up shares for quite modest amounts.

Clearly then, if we have to pay out thousands of pounds every time we want to buy shares, it is going to stop large numbers of people investing in the stock market.

But all is not lost. Our forefathers ran up against the same problems years ago, and they decided to develop what are known as 'collective investments'. You might not have heard of the name 'collective investments' but you could well have heard of the two types of collective investment most commonly used – 'unit trusts' and 'investment trusts'.

Despite their names and the use of the word 'trust', the two types of investment are very different. Their only common feature is that they both collectively invest in shares.

They are both pooled arrangements where you, I, and others, put our money into a pool in order to buy shares. It is a good arrangement because the trust can now afford to buy shares in lots of £5,000 or £10,000 and spread the costs among us.

These collective investments are an ideal way of putting

small amounts of money into the stock market.

There is another aspect to this pooled arrangement. Naturally, if you pool your money, not only will you be able to spread the cost of buying, but you also spread the risk.

You might not be able to put £100,000 into ten different shares – but your unit or investment trust might be able to. If you can spread your exposure to ten different shares then if one goes badly wrong, at least the other nine will help soften the blow.

This is exactly what happens with collective investments and as we shall see, their performance, whether it be a unit or investment trust, is linked not to one or two shares, but often large numbers of shares, all of which are 'managed' on your behalf, for which you pay management charges.

There is one other aspect of unit and investment trusts which also makes them ideally suited for the small investor – or indeed any investor who is either not interested in or does not have time for monitoring the stock market – and that is, they can usually be bought through a 'savings plan'.

Now, if you are happy with the concept of saving regularly, then by your very nature you will tend to be a long-term saver. Certainly, whether you buy into either unit or investment trusts then you have to regard yourself as a long-term saver – and by 'long term' I would say an absolute minimum of three years, and more like five years.

But saving into a unit or investment trust has other positive aspects of which you should also be aware. Normally, if you were buying shares, then you would want to buy when the price is low and sell when the price is high. The same applies to unit and investment trusts to the extent that you would not want to invest in the stock market if the newspapers are full of doom and gloom about the possibility of a stock market collapse.

Having said that, savings plans totally disregard what is going on in the stock market – you simply keep on putting your money in regardless. Apart from not having to worry about the timing of your investment, the ups and downs of the stock market can have a beneficial effect on your savings plan.

When the market is booming the cost of stock that you buy in your unit or investment trust is high and so each month you buy small amounts at a time. However, when the market falls, your fixed regular monthly premium buys a larger amount of stock. When the market picks up again, the value of your holding, which grew more rapidly in size when the market was depressed, suddenly becomes more valuable as the price of the underlying stock increases.

This phenomenon experienced by regular savers is called 'pound cost averaging' – an almost mystical concept which benefits the investor who chooses regular savings plans.

TEN

Unit Trusts

So what is so good about unit trusts?

Unit trusts provide one of the best and cheapest ways of investing in the stock market.

In terms of long-term performance they have outstripped not only the Retail Prices Index, but also National Savings certificates, bank deposit and building society deposit accounts – and the differences are quite marked .

If you take the example of £1,000 invested in an average trust in the UK General sector the comparative figures for the different types of investment over five, ten and 15 years would have been as follows:

	5 years	10 years	15 years
Unit trust	2,576	6,036	14,744
Bank	1,256	1,769	2,220
Building society	1,520	2,388	3,513
National Savings	1,444	2,355	3,367
Retail Prices Index	1,293	2,101	4,216

(*Source:* The Unit Trust Association, July 1, 1989.)

How do unit trusts work?

When a unit trust is set up, it will usually be designed to fulfil a given objective. That objective may be to invest in British shares to achieve capital growth, or it may be to invest in the shares of, say, American or Japanese smaller companies.

That objective will hopefully attract investors to the trust, once they have been invited to subscribe for units. The management group will advertise widely, quoting a price for the units of, say, 50p each.

Investors attracted to the new trust may in total put, say, £30m into the trust during the 'offer period' which usually lasts some weeks. This £30m will create 60m units and the money will be invested in shares which the managers believe will achieve the stated objective.

If the unit trust invests all £30m at the start of its first day – once the offer period has been closed – and the value of the shares rise by 10 per cent, then the management group will put up the value of the units by ten per cent. Your 50p unit would therefore now be worth 55p.

But unit trusts do not sit still. New investors might, on the second day, be attracted to the new trust. If they now want to buy units then they would have to pay 55p for them. With this new money coming in, the unit trust manager simply creates new units and invests the proceeds. By the end of the second day, the number of units issued by the new trust may have risen from 60 million units to, say, 61 million.

This is, in essence, how unit trusts work. The unit price goes up and down as the value of the underlying investments goes up and down. To make money the value of your units has to rise – you lose if the value of the units fall.

How unit trusts provide an income

If you have previously invested in shares, then you would know that companies pay a 'dividend' – usually twice a year by cheque. This dividend is the reward the shareholder gets for investing in the company.

With a unit trust, the unit trust management group collects all these dividends and re-distributes the money to you, the unit holder, in the form of 'income'. This income has nothing to do with your investment rising and falling in value; it relates strictly to the dividends paid out by companies on the underlying shares.

Some unit trusts managers put your money into companies which promise a good and steadily rising dividend payment. This objective will result in a higher than average dividend payment and so this type of trust – an income trust – is a handy investment if you need an income from your investment. And because the value of the company shares can rise in value, you should also see the value of your shares rise.

It is for this reason that investors are prepared to take a risk in the stock market. For, while your deposit account will provide an income in terms of the interest paid, your actual investment will not rise in value.

Not everyone wants to receive an income from their unit trust investment. They simply want to see their capital grow in value. In this case, you, the investor would put your money in a 'growth' trust whose objective was to invest solely in companies whose share price was expected to rise substantially, but whose dividend payments could well be low.

You may well, therefore, see a unit trust advertised suggesting you put your money into the XYZ Japanese Growth Trust, or the ABC British Income Fund.

Some trusts are more risky than others. For example those described as a 'special situations' fund or 'smaller company' fund will tend to be more risky than a 'general' fund.

Some unit trusts investing in particular areas might be more risky than others. For example, a Far Eastern Special Situations Trust, or an Australian Gold Fund, would be more risky than a UK or Japanese General Fund.

So there is a hierarchy of risk. Most would-be unit trust investors begin by investing at home – in the UK – so perhaps the only major decision which has to be made is whether to go for an income or capital growth trust.

In recent years, UK income trusts have done very well – not only have they produced a regular income, but they have also seen good capital growth.

So if you hanker to buy into an income trust you can do so even though you might not want the income. Some trusts allow you simply to reinvest the income to buy more units, while others have different types of unit to suit customer needs.

If you do want your income to accumulate within the fund then you simply buy 'accumulation units' – which form part of a separate fund – and the management group automatically adjusts the value of your units upwards. Accumulation units are, therefore, more valuable than income units.

How do I choose?

The first problem you find when choosing a unit trust is that there is a lot of them to choose from. Apart from the different types – income, growth, special situations etc – you also have trusts investing in different countries – UK, American, Pacific, Europe, or International.

Each unit trust falls into one of these 'sectors'. You should get to know basically what these sectors have to offer. For example, UK general trusts invest in mainly UK shares covering several industries in order to provide steady growth in income and capital.

UK growth trusts differ in that their priority is to go for companies whose share price is likely to grow quickly, while UK income trusts go for companies whose income is likely to increase.

You should seek descriptions of the exact definition of each sector from the specialist magazines before making your choice or, failing that, write to the Unit Trust Association at 65 Kingsway, London WC2B 6TD.

There are new types of unit trust. For example, you can have a money market unit trust, which invests solely in cash funds such as those managed by banks and building societies.

In case you are wondering why unit trusts should invest in deposit accounts, it is because these funds can get a better rate of interest than your humble bank account, because they deal in such large sums. Such trusts are easy and efficient if you want to 'park' your money should you want to move out of a particular sector for a short time.

You can even get a unit trust which invests only in other unit trusts – the ultimate way of spreading your risk!

Once you have narrowed your own investment objectives to a particular sector, how do you then choose a particular management group?

Many types of financial institution run unit trusts. Some of these you may have heard of because they also provide insurance – such as Prudential, Pearl, Commercial Union, Legal & General, and Scottish Amicable – and there are those who are specialist 'fund managers' such as M&G, Fidelity, Save & Prosper, Henderson, and Gartmore.

Then there are banks which run unit trusts – such as Barclays, TSB and Lloyds – and those known for their stockbroking and merchant banking expertise – James Capel, Morgan Grenfell and Kleinwort Benson. There are those run by companies which provide an all-round financial planning and investment service, such as Hill Samuel.

But how do you choose one from the other? If you want to maximize your returns, the only real way of choosing one fund from another is by looking at their 'past performance'.

Look at it this way. If you were to choose which football club was likely to win a Cup Final then you are likely to choose one which has done well in the past, rather than one which traditionally has been a poor performer.

So it is with unit trusts. While past performance does not guarantee future rewards, it does provide an indication of the expertise of the trust's manager.

If you want to compare past performance then there are two ways of doing it: either you go along to an independent financial adviser to seek help or look yourself.

There is not much point going to a company representative – he can only sell you his company's products – and that is not much good if his particular trust has been at the bottom of the league for some time.

If you want to do it yourself, then you will have to go out and buy one of the specialist financial magazines, such as Money Management, Planned Savings, or What Investment?

At the end of these magazines you will find a mass of tables which give the performance of the trusts over different periods of time – one month, three months, one year, two years, three years, five years and ten years, depending on which magazine you choose.

These tables will show not only how much a particular trust has grown in value over a particular period, but how well a trust has done when compared to others in its sector.

And just because a trust is the number one performer over ten years, does not mean it is doing very well over, say, one year. You need to identify a trust which has been a 'consistent' performer – not some fly-by-night fund.

If the tables show that there are, say, 80 funds in your chosen sector, and you spot a fund which has never been lower than 20 over the different time periods, then you have spotted a fund which has consistently been in the top 25 per cent of its sector over those periods.

If you spot a fund which one minute is high in the tables over one particular period then plummets to the bottom, then you had best look elsewhere. This is the sort of fund which has not been consistent, and by investing in it, you might find you do so when it is on one of its traditional downward trends.

While this is the best way of spotting funds you can also supplement this knowledge with what you read in the newspapers. For example, every now and again, the national newspapers write on the best performing management group – the group whose funds as a whole saw the best increase in value.

So if you cannot decide which of two funds to choose by looking at the tables, then choose the one whose management group is rated highly.

How to buy and sell unit trusts

Buying and selling unit trusts is fairly simple and straightforward. Two prices are quoted by the management group – the buying price and the selling price.

The higher price quoted is the buying or 'offer' price, while the lower price is the selling or 'bid' price. The difference between the bid and offer price is called the 'spread' and it represents the cost of investing in the unit trust.

In order to make a profit, the price of your units must rise at least from the bid to the offer price quoted on the day you invested. You have to cover your costs with a rise in value before your investment begins to grow.

You should be aware that this making up of ground to cover the spread can be quite wide – as much as 11 per cent. However, most groups try to keep the spread down to six per cent, and you should take special note of any with a narrower spread, as this represents better value for money.

You may also, in some newspapers, come across what is known as the 'cancellation price'. If you become interested in unit trusts then you will need to know more about cancellation prices – the lowest price you get when you sell – but to avoid confusion you should, initially at least, concentrate on the bid and offer prices.

When you see unit trust literature, you should always look at the cost of investing. The 'initial' cost, which is covered by the spread, will always be quoted. A second cost, representing the annual management fee, will also be spelled out. This is usually lower than the initial charge, but is one which recurs year in, year out. Again take special note, when choosing a trust, of those whose annual charge is lower.

Charges at present range from around 1.25 per cent to 1.5 per cent per year. The lower the charge, the more money left invested in units.

One of the problems for the unit trust investor is that you may not know exactly how many units you are buying when you first invest. This is because the price quoted in your newspaper may not be the price at which you can deal.

Personally, I do not think you should worry too much about this, as by the time you make your investment the price could well have changed.

If you do want to buy or sell, then you can telephone or write to your management group or get your adviser to do it for you. You can also respond to advertisements in your newspaper. The financial magazines often have the names and addresses of the management groups, as well as telephone numbers.

Once you have put in an order to buy units you will be issued with a 'contract note' within 24 hours. Once you have paid for your purchase you will then be sent a registration certificate, but beware, this could take between three weeks and three months to arrive.

You will need to send the registration certificate back to the unit trust group should you sell, as this represents proof of ownership.

If you want to keep track of your unit trust then the bid/offer spread will be quoted daily in leading national newspapers, and often weekly in others. All you need to do is to multiply the number of units you own by the bid price.

What about tax?

If you are a non-taxpayer then unit trusts are a particularly worthwhile investment, especially if you want an extra source of income. This is because you can reclaim the tax which has already been deducted when you receive your dividend income.

They are particularly useful, therefore, if your husband is a taxpayer and you are not – or vice versa. By putting the unit trust investments into your name you can maximize your income from your unit trust investment until you have used up all your allowance.

If you are in the position where your partner holds unit trusts, then get him – or her – to transfer them into your name in order to make the best of your allowance.

Basic rate taxpayers should not have to worry too much about the tax on income from the unit trust because the management group has paid the tax on your behalf.

Similarly, if you are a higher rate taxpayer, then, as with deposit accounts, you will be called upon to top up on the amount of tax you pay to the Inland Revenue from your unit trust income.

As far as capital gains tax is concerned, then you are liable to pay it on your investment gains – subject to using up your annual allowance, which in the 1989-90 tax year is £5,000.

Lump sum, savings plans and portfolios

When buying unit trusts you will find that each management group has a minimum figure which can be invested. This figure could be as high as £2,000 or as low as £25, depending on the group and the trust in which you want to invest.

The same applies to savings plans – it is obviously not worth a unit trust company collecting, say, £1 a month, so around £25 should be treated as a minimum figure.

Unit trusts are also a good idea for those with much more money to spend. This is particularly true for those who can not be too bothered about checking their investments and would prefer someone else to do the leg work for them.

For example, if you had £10,000 to invest in unit trusts then you would want to spread your money and risk, among two, three or perhaps more trusts. But in what proportion?

Many unit trust groups run portfolio management services which simply means they put your money into more than one unit trust and then move the money around as market conditions dictate. Each portfolio has an objective – often either divided between getting a good income or getting capital growth.

What is good about this approach to investment is that the manager – who has his or her ear much closer to the ground than you or I – will fine tune the spread of the investment in order to balance quite finely risk and reward.

When times get rough the manager will not be able to generate as much capital growth or income without taking greater risk. The manager will spot such occasions and be able quickly to reduce your exposure to risk by moving into safer waters – though performance is bound to suffer. Without such an approach we laymen might not spot the coming storm, and then get hard hit when we fail to take cover.

The problem of the portfolio management approach is that it does usually cost more because you are getting an extra tier of management. Arguably, though, if you do have a lot to invest and you are simply not interested in the nuts and bolts of investment, then the portfolio approach is for you.

Unit trusts vs the rest

When comparing unit trusts against endowment policies you always run up against the fact that when an insurance company pays a bonus they cannot take it back, so what you make you hold on to.

This is not the case with unit trusts. Units can go down as

well as up. However, to cover themselves, insurance companies have to take more conservative 'guesstimates' when providing bonuses, so naturally performance tends to be 'slow but sure'. When things go well, unit trusts can far outstrip the performance of endowments, particularly if the investment is a long-term one.

And because units can be bought and sold easily, they are much more of a flexible investment than endowments. Early encashment of an endowment can lead to heavy losses.

When it comes to insurance bonds, unit trusts do not have to pay capital gains tax on gains within the funds – insurance companies, on the other hand, have to pay CGT for gains within the bond funds.

Regular 'savers' in a unit-linked insurance bond will, however, not be liable to CGT on the proceeds, whereas unit trust holders will be – that is a disincentive then for higher rate taxpayers. It is only lump sum investors among the higher rate taxpayers who are liable to pay CGT on the proceeds from bonds.

Then we have the unit trust movement's great rivals – the investment trusts; more about them in the next chapter.

ELEVEN

Investment Trusts

A better deal for your money?

Investment trusts are a completely different animal from their like-sounding counterparts, the unit trusts.

Until recently, they have also not been as popular. Some say this is because they are a rather complex animal, others say that it is because they are not allowed to advertise.

Whatever the truth, investment trusts are worth considering particularly as they were originally set-up over 100 years ago as a way for the small investor to go into the stock market cheaply.

And there is no doubt that in recent times, the popularity of the investment trust has grown. The advent of saving schemes – which somewhat perversely, can be advertised – has given the investment trusts something of a higher profile.

So what are they? Investment trusts are 'quoted' companies – in other words, their shares are traded on the International Stock Exchange in London.

But, unlike other companies they do not manufacture anything, they do not mine or process or provide services. Rather, an investment trust is a company whose sole aim in life is to invest its shareholders' money.

You do not buy units in an investment trust, you buy shares. And unlike units in a unit trust, the manager does not create shares every time an investor puts in more money. As with all quoted companies, investment trusts have only a certain number of shares in issue at any one time.

This inevitably means that when the shares are sought after, the price rises, and when they are less popular, the price falls. Generally, supply and demand play big parts in determining the value of a company's share and investment trusts are no exception.

As with a unit trust, the investment trust company is run by a team of experts who, hopefully, are good at investing money. The money they raise when the investment trust company is initially launched is used to invest in the shares of other companies in much the same way as a unit holder's money is invested by a unit trust.

When investment trusts were originally launched it was because small investors needed a way of spreading their savings among a larger number of shares in order to reduce risk. They also sought the professional management that the investment trust solution could provide.

They were also concerned about cost, but realized that the cost of running the investment trust could be off-set by the income it made. Nowadays, the annual management charges run to just 0.5 per cent, which compares very favourably with unit trusts, who generally charge between 1 and 1.5 per cent per year.

They have another advantage over unit trusts and that is they do not have to restrict themselves to investing their money in companies quoted on the Stock Exchange. They could, if they wish, invest in up-and-coming companies which have not been going long enough to have obtained a stock market quote.

This ability to move into unquoted investments has helped the average investment trust perform a bit better than the average unit trust because, traditionally, unit trusts can only invest in quoted companies.

According to the independent statistics company, Micropal, up until the end of July 1989, the average investment trust would have turned £100 invested over the previous 12 months into £136.50p, while the average unit trust would have turned it into £120.20p. Over five years, £100 would have been worth £304.50p in the average investment trust against £250.10p in the average unit trust.

Investment trusts are, therefore, well worth considering as a way of going into the stock market.

How do investment trusts work?

You will remember I said that some people felt that investment trusts were a 'rather complicated animal': any misunderstanding of the way they work comes from their very nature.

Because investment trusts invest primarily in the shares of other companies, you would expect that if you added up all the values of the investment trust's shares the figure you arrived at would represent the value of the company.

Sadly, this is not the case. Because the investment trust company's shares are influenced by the supply and demand for them, then the value of the company may be more or less than the value of its underlying investments – its 'assets'.

Where the investment trust's shares are worth more than the total value of the underlying assets the shares are said to stand at a 'premium' but if it is the other way around, then the shares stand at a 'discount'.

If you buy investment trust company shares when they stand at a discount, you might invest £1,000 but the actual value of the underlying assets might actually be worth £1,200.

The fact that you can invest £1 to pick up assets worth £1.20p has not gone unnoticed. Some large companies have taken over investment trusts simply to realize the value of their underlying assets by selling them.

If this happens while you are a shareholder you could find that you suddenly get a good offer for your shares, in which case you might decide to sell them to the bidding company.

For practical reasons then, the 'premium' and the 'discount' should only really concern you if an offer is made for your investment trust company.

How do investment trusts provide an income?

Investment trusts pay dividends in much the same way as any other quoted company pays a dividend. The company makes money, takes out its costs, and then gives some of what is left to its shareholders.

However, in recent years many investment trust companies have restructured themselves in order to provide a better choice for investors.

Not every investor wants to take an income; some prefer just to see a capital gain, still others prefer a mixture of the two. A unit trust group can manage to meet these objectives by setting up different trusts to cover differing objectives – an investment trust company has to take a different road in order to do the same.

Investment trusts do this by converting themselves into 'split-capital' trusts. Quite simply, a split-level trust enables the investor either to take an income or take the capital growth.

The simplest split-level trust, therefore, has two types of share – 'income' and 'capital' shares. The income shares attract all the income made by the investment trust company, while the capital shares get all the capital growth.

In order to distribute both capital and income the split-level trust has to be wound up at a predetermined date. In simple terms, once this date is reached, the managers look at how much income has been made, and give that to the holders of the income shares, and then how much capital has been gained, and give that to the holders of the capital shares.

The income-generating shares are, therefore, ideal for the investor who wants a rising income – perhaps in retirement – while the capital shares might be ideal for someone saving for retirement who does not need the income.

If you are a first-time investor in investment trusts then you are unlikely to want to invest in anything other than in what has just been described. However, you should be aware of other aspects of split-capital investment trusts which are designed to meet special needs.

For example, some companies have 'stepped preference' shares, which provide a predetermined entitlement to both capital and income growth. Then there are 'zero dividend preference shares', which have a fixed date for repayment at a predetermined amount. They pay no dividend because the income is effectively reinvested into the capital value.

And finally there are 'warrants', which entitle the holder to buy a fixed number of ordinary or capital shares at a pre-determined price over a set period. The warrants do not have to be exercised if you do not want to.

Seek help when choosing an investment trust

Picking an investment trust is no easy matter. Unlike the unit trusts, the specialist financial magazines do not pay the same close attention to investment trust performance figures as they do to unit trust figures.

For this reason alone, the small investor should seek the help of an adviser if you like the idea of investment trusts.

In choosing an investment trust you and your adviser will look, as you might with a unit trust, into the various different sectors – each of which has its own risk profile.

The Association of Investment Trust Companies, which is based at 16 Finsbury Circus, London EC2M 7JU, divides investment companies into 13 different categories.

Like unit trusts, there is a 'general' category whose aim is to provide capital income and growth, while a number of international categories, including the 'UK' category, are aimed at just growth.

Then there is an income growth sector, a smaller companies sector, special features sector and the split-level trusts which I talked about earlier.

You have to be very careful as to which category you choose to invest in. For example, some trusts might invest in commodities or energy – areas which are highly volatile and therefore very risky.

As with unit trusts, past performance is one of the main ways of looking at the various investment trusts. You can do so simply by looking at the past performance of the company's share price. A stockbroker and a minority of independent financial advisers can do this for you.

They can also show you how to compare investment trusts by looking at how well the managers have invested your money. This is done by looking at the return they have made on capital invested. What your adviser will look for is the rate of growth in the size of the investment trust's assets.

There are good reasons for looking at both measurements. For example, with split-level trusts, the share price of capital shares will rise quite steeply as the redemption date comes around – so a good showing in the performance of the share price need not necessarily show that the managers have done well.

Another measure of an investment trust's performance is to adopt one method used by the unit trust groups – to compare the performance of your investment trust with that of other similar investment trusts.

Choosing an investment trust is therefore not an easy task, so your best bet is to leave the choosing to an adviser – once you have told him what you want from your investment.

Buying and selling the shares is very straightforward. The share price is quoted in the quality newspapers so you have some indication of the previous day's value. If you want to buy or sell you simply get hold of your stockbroker.

What about taxation?

There is no difference in the way you pay tax on investment trusts from the way you pay it on ordinary shares and unit trusts.

As far as income tax is concerned, the non-taxpayer has the ability to reclaim the tax that has been deducted at source by the company before your dividend is paid.

The basic rate taxpayer does not have to worry about paying income tax, as it has already been deducted. And in the case of the higher rate taxpayer, you simply have to take account of the additional income and ensure that you pay more income tax at a rate which equals the difference between the basic and higher rates, at the end of the tax year.

With capital gains tax you have two concessions. First there is the fact that your first few thousand pounds of gains are tax free. In the 1989-90 tax year, the allowance was £5,000.

Then there is the question of indexation. Before you actually hand over your money to the taxman, you have to take into account inflation on the gain, deduct it from your 'gain' and then calculate CGT at your personal rate. This is helped by using indexation tables supplied by the Inland Revenue.

As will be discussed later, you can hold your investment trust holdings within a Personal Equity Plan to make them more tax efficient. You will find more about PEPs later (see chapter 13).

Investment trusts vs the rest

In many respects the arguments used when comparing investment trusts with other investments such as endowment policies and insurance bonds are very much the same as I described in the previous chapter when discussing unit trusts.

But there is no doubt that the investment trusts movement's greatest rival is the unit trust industry. As investment trusts become more orientated towards attracting the smaller investor, they have to grit their teeth while the unit trust groups advertise their wares to the general public.

Investment trust management groups are not allowed to advertise their trusts because companies are not allowed to advertise their shares for fear of creating a 'false market'. As the laws of supply and demand do not affect unit trusts, there is nothing standing in their way when they want to advertise their products.

To a certain extent, the investment trust industry has got around this problem by advertising its savings schemes. Nowadays many investment trusts have savings schemes which work very much like the unit trust savings schemes and they have the same advantages, such as pound cost averaging.

Such schemes can be advertised quite legally by the investment trust groups and they are doing so quite heavily.

But there are other – and more important – differences between the investment trusts and the unit trusts which might benefit you the investor.

Probably the most important is that it is generally cheaper to invest in investment trusts than unit trusts, though this does vary according to the size of your transaction and whether you invest through a lump sum or a savings plan.

It is performance which really counts at the end of the day and there is no doubt that investment trusts have, on average, done better than unit trusts.

However, that is no reason why you should choose investment trusts rather than unit trusts. My advice would be that if you cannot fully grasp the way in which investment trusts work, then look to unit trusts even though your return might not be quite as good.

It is better to invest in something that you fully understand so that you can manage your investments properly, than put your money into something whose subtleties you cannot grasp and which becomes unmanageable.

TWELVE

Raising the Stakes – Investing in Shares

Risk and reward

Given that there are some very good reasons why small investors should go into unit or investment trusts you might wonder why some nine million investors in the UK want to put their money directly into shares.

After all, shares are a much riskier investment option, because you ignore what should be a prime objective, and that is to spread your money around.

One of the ways around this problem is to do just that and invest lots of money, spreading it among a large number of different companies in order to achieve the same objective as collective investment.

Unfortunately, in order to do that you would need to invest an absolute minimum of around £10,000 – and £20,000 probably comes closer to the mark. Not all of us can afford to do that.

So why then go into shares (or 'equities' as they are sometimes called) at all? The reason is quite simple – *the greater the risk, the greater the reward*. And, for those who are really interested in the stock market, it can also be good fun – providing, that is, you are prepared to take the risks involved.

Let us have a look at some figures to illustrate just how well shares have done over the past few years.

There are a number of ways to show how the UK stock market as a whole has grown over the years, but one of the best measures for the 'collective' rise in equities is the 'FT All

Share Index', which covers a large number of equities on the stock market.

The following figures from the Unit Trust Association compares the value of the index, five ten and 15 years ago, and compares them with the average unit trust in the UK General and UK Growth sectors as at July 1, 1989.

	5 years	10 years	15 years
UK General	2693	10,572	28,657
UK Growth	2630	9343	24,789
FTA Index	2538	9655	27,959

As you can see, the UK General unit trusts tended to 'out perform' the FT All Share Index, while the UK Growth sector did not.

What you do not see is that some unit trusts at the bottom of the UK General sector did not beat the 'index' while some at the top of the UK Growth sector probably did, and the same applies to the UK General sector.

But more to the point, individual shares which make up the FT All Share Index would have done much better than the best performing unit trusts and some would have done much worse.

So where does that leave us the investor? The fact is that because some shares do extremely well, and out-perform the index, there is always the temptation to try to identify such shares and invest in them before they begin their upward spiral of growth. And there is no doubt that if you do spot them you can do very well indeed.

However, it is not easy to choose the winners, given that there is a whole army of professional investors – including the managers of investment and unit trusts – to compete against. Remember that for every buyer there is a seller, and vice versa – this means that for every winner there is sure to be a loser.

It has to be said, therefore, that unless you are prepared to spend a great deal of time studying the stock market then you are unlikely to get rich quick.

So what should be your objective? Firstly, you would want your money to provide a better long-term return than it would in a deposit account. After all, that is why you want to put your money into shares.

Then you would want your selected stocks to perform better than unit and investments trusts. If you did not then it would hardly be worth moving away from collective investments.

And while you would like to see your holdings increase in value, you would have to assess as best you can how much risk you can afford to take. And finally you would want to decide whether your investments should veer towards achieving good capital growth or towards the generation of an income.

Once you have made these decisions then the type of shares you are likely to buy begins to emerge. For example, if you want to generate some additional income, then you would not choose a small company in a sector which traditionally tends to pay a low dividend.

However, you might want to go for such a company if you feel you can afford to take a risk and are seeking a rapid rise in capital growth.

So your objectives to a large extent should dictate the sort of share you should buy.

How to reduce the risks

When you invest in shares you face not only the risks faced by the individual company in which you have a share, but also the risk faced by the 'sector' that the company is in, as well as the risks faced by the market as a whole.

You no doubt will have seen news stories on the television about a particular company saying something like, 'millions of pounds were wiped of the value of X company today when such and such foreign government pulled out of a deal to supply spare parts for its armed forces'.

The fact is that individual companies are exposed to a whole series of risks which can affect their trading pattern. Generally speaking, you should try to pick a company which

108

you feel is unlikely to have such problems and yet promises good growth for the future. But this is not easy. For example, few realised in 1989 that the 'salmonella in eggs' scare would seriously affect the performance of some food companies.

Then there are the risks faced by individual sectors. Every company listed on the stock market is put into a sector. If you look in a newspaper such as the Financial Times you will find a sector which contains all the banks, then there are the 'motor' sector and the 'electrical' sector.

But sectors also face risks. For example, if there is a sharp downturn in the property market then all those companies which own estate agency chains will be adversely affected. If a large number of, say, insurance companies have estate agency chains, then it will act to bring down the value of the sector as a whole.

This, to a large extent, is what happened to the banking sector in the second half of the 1980s. A combination of stiff competition and problems associated with lending too much money to the developing world, all helped depress the sector.

Finally we have problems which hit the whole market. A bad set of trade figures, as you will know from watching the news on television, will wipe millions off of the value of shares, so will news of rising inflation.

In order to reduce risk, therefore, you have to avoid putting your money into companies who are likely to be hit by various factors. Actually spotting these factors is another matter.

You can do this by spreading the purchase of your shares among a number of companies in different sectors, and put some in foreign companies listed on the UK Stock Exchange, all of which helps to reduce risk.

Looking for a bargain

If you were buying oranges rather than shares, then you would know that there were times when you felt oranges were a bargain, and times when they were rather expensive.

This is because the value of oranges in the market place tends to fluctuate with the seasons. The fruit market has managed to iron out a lot of the peaks and troughs in the supply of oranges to the UK, but there will be times when you feel that some of those oranges are just not as good as you had earlier in the year.

Shares are also bought in the market – the stock market. And, just like oranges, their value fluctuates. The cost of shares will rise steadily as a company grows; whether you think the share is 'good value' or not is another matter.

Of course, if you are buying oranges you get a feel for the market, and you know which fruits and vegetables represent good value. Unfortunately, it is not so easy with shares, though there are some simple points to watch out for.

Probably the worst time to invest in shares is when everyone is saying what a great place the stock market is to put your money. When the stock market is rising quickly, just like a crate of oranges, the point comes where it gets too costly and the price inevitably falls.

It is like shopping. The best time to get into the stock market is during the 'Spring sales' – not the Christmas rush!

But how do you know when shares are cheap to buy?

There are two ways open to the small investor. First, you can spot opportunities. If we have a fantastically hot summer, then ice cream sales will go up, just as sales of umbrellas go up if we have a wet summer.

If a company gives what appear to you to be good reasons for taking over another company, there again its sales and, we hope, its profits will also climb.

When sales climb, providing this can be achieved without a huge rise in costs, then the company will make more profits, and you the shareholder will own a slightly larger slice of the profits than you did before.

This means that the profits – otherwise known as 'earnings' – can be divided by the number of shares in circulation to give a figure which represents how much profit can be ascribed to each share. 'Earnings per share' is a useful figure to watch because it shows just how much of the profits are being earned by each of your shares.

Of course, if your ten shares in the Blockbuster Drains

Company see an increase in Earnings Per Share because the company is making more profits, then the shares become more valuable, and so the stock market price is likely to rise.

Just like the oranges, the shares in Blockbuster have increased in value because investors feel they are now more valuable than before.

But how do you know whether Blockbuster's shares are cheap or expensive?

If you were buying oranges and you saw the price of oranges rise sharply when the price of apples, pears and bananas did not change, then you would begin to think that oranges were no longer good value.

So it is with shares. If Blockbuster Drain Company's shares seem out of step with other drain companies in its sector – then you would not buy.

Unfortunately, you cannot judge whether Blockbuster's shares are cheap or expensive simply by looking at its share price and comparing one share price with another – that is irrelevant as far as we are concerned.

However, there is a way of spotting whether Blockbuster looks cheap when set alongside it rival drain company.

What you need to do is to pick up a pencil and paper and write down Blockbuster's current share price – which is found in the back of your newspaper. Then look at the Earnings Per Share, from the most recent statement about the company's profits, and divide one into the other.

The answer represents what is known in that foreign language, Cityspeak, as the 'price earnings ratio', or more simply the 'PE'.

If you do the same for Blockbuster's rival, you can then compare the two PEs.

If Blockbuster's PE is much higher than its rival's then that can be interpreted that it is 'rated' highly by the stock market. It usually means that while Blockbuster is doing well it has the potential to do even better, so increasing earnings in the future.

The greater the esteem in which the company is held, the higher the PE ratio. So if you look at the banking sector and you see a PE which is out of line with the rest, then it is because that share is for some reason rated more highly than the others.

If you felt that one of the more lowly rated shares in a sector deserved a higher rating – perhaps because new management had just been put into the company – then you might want to buy the share because you feel that there is a potential for an upward re-rating. In other words you feel the share is cheap relative to others in the sector; this presents an opportunity to buy.

Thankfully, you do not have to get out a pen and paper and calculate PEs these days. If you look in the back of the Financial Times and look at the share prices, you will see that all the PEs are worked out for you alongside the share price. Spotting good value is therefore made less difficult.

Having said that, spotting a bargain has to be done in conjunction with all your other research on a company and the newspapers are as good a place as any to do that.

Watching the market

It is clear then, that in order to achieve anything out of the stock market you have to keep a close eye on what is going on. The one obvious way of doing this is to keep a close eye on the quality newspapers and specialist magazines.

The Financial Times covers virtually every company, particularly when they make announcements via the Stock Exchange.

The other quality dailies also cover a large number of companies, particularly The Times, Independent, Daily Telegraph, and The Guardian. You could also look to your local regional newspapers if they have city papers.

The 'regionals' quite often spot an investment opportunity simply because they tend to keep a close eye on their local companies – companies which the national newspapers might not be so interested in, often because they are smaller than some of the better-known names.

One consequence of the national newspapers' putting greater emphasis on the very large companies is that the top

100 companies in size – the 'Top 100' – will be covered regularly. From the first-time investor's point of view, these are the stocks which should form a 'core' holding – the main shares – in your collection.

The specialist magazines should be bought if you are serious about investing in the stockmarket. The Investor's Chronicle is particularly useful.

By keeping a firm eye on the newspapers and magazines you can keep a firm eye on what the companies get up to. Most companies report their progress twice a year – after the first six months of their financial year, known as the 'interim' stage, and at the end of the year when the 'final' results are announced.

All announcements first go through the Stock Exchange via its computerized announcement service, TOPIC, on which are glued the eyes of thousands of professional fund managers waiting to make instant decisions as they react to every snippet of news.

This instant reaction to announcements is another good reason for steering clear of equities. The professionals have all the tools of their trade at their fingertips – you don't!

However, you can try to guess what is likely to happen – the professionals do. For example, if you come across a company whose trading performance is pretty mediocre, but has one or two attractive subsidiaries, then that company could be taken-over.

If the situation arises and you hold shares in that company, then the value of your shares is almost certain to rise. The bidding company will ask you to part with your shares at a certain price, and you have to decide whether to part with them or not.

If every shareholder decides to part with them, then the bidding company wins control of your old company and, hopefully, you will have made a decent profit on your investment.

Market sentiment plays a big part. When Jaguar announced in September 1989 that its profits were well down the value of Jaguar shares fell sharply, even though the possibility of its being taken over within around 18 months was on the cards.

A few days later the giant US car maker Ford declared its intention to buy up to 15 per cent of Jaguar and the shares rocketed in value again.

New managements, new products, new markets, can all help push up a company's share price – it is up to you to spot them before these factors have a positive impact on the company's performance.

Buying and selling

In much the same way as the independent financial advisers advise on and sell insurance products, so stockbrokers buy and sell shares - and charge you for doing so.

Because a minimum charge is always made, it is not worth your while dealing in small numbers of shares – it simply is uneconomical.

However, some stockbrokers, and indeed other institutions, have tackled this problem by separating the buying and selling functions of the stockbroker from the advisory function.

By offering 'execution only' services, some stockbrokers have managed to keep their prices down, although they still work on a minimum sale.

You really have to shop around to find the best deal. You might find that your bank or building society deal in shares and their charges might better suit your pocket than your local stockbroker.

On the other hand, some stockbrokers have set up very comprehensive dealing systems which you buy and sell through, again without having to pay for a more personal tailored service.

Execution-only services are fine if you are confident that you have a grasp of the stock market. However, if you can afford to enlist the advisory services of a stockbroker, then you should do so.

Stockbrokers also offer portfolio management services – in other words, they look after your shares for you, and make the investment decisions. Again, this is an ideal service if you can afford it, but the obvious alternative is to go into a collective investment.

You could also come across opportunities to buy shares through your job. Many companies operate 'save as you earn' share option schemes.

This is simply a savings scheme which gives you the option after five or seven years to buy your company's shares at a price fixed in advance. If your company is an up and coming operation, then these schemes can be very lucrative indeed.

Another option is the 'approved profit sharing scheme' which enables your company to set aside profits to buy shares on your behalf.

THIRTEEN

Personal Equity Plans

Stockmarket investments – tax and the PEPs revolution

When former Chancellor of the Exchequer, Nigel Lawson, introduced Personal Equity Plans in 1987, they were hailed by some as a revolutionary scheme to encourage the growth of wider share ownership.

And many in the financial services industry saw an opportunity to sell a brand new product which effectively provided a mini- tax haven for those who were prepared to invest in the stock market.

In particular, the unit trust providers felt there was an opportunity to encourage collective investment and so they went about putting PEPs together, despite the complex system of rules devised to ensure the Inland Revenue retained control over their new pet.

However, the rules were onerous so management groups were not too keen on them, and the benefits to the investor were so heavily qualified that many felt they were not really an attractive proposition.

But then the old-style PEPs were dealt a body blow from which they were never to recover. The stock market crash of 1987 so destroyed the once hitherto raging enthusiasm of the newly won stock market investor, that the PEP idea withered on the vine.

Throughout 1988 investor confidence continued at a low ebb, and some of those unit trust groups that had decided to join in and launch PEPs – albeit somewhat reluctantly because of the stifling rules – finally decided to pull out.

By the time Mr Lawson rose to his feet in the House of

Commons to present his 1989 Budget, the Government had come under intense pressure to smarten up the PEPs scheme and allow the collective investment schemes to have a greater say.

To a certain extent, Mr Lawson gave them what they wanted. PEPs became much simpler for the manager to administer, and became more attractive from the investor's point of view because more money could be put into collective investments rather than directly into more volatile stocks and shares.

So what is a PEP?

A Personal Equity Plan is simply a vehicle to allow you to invest in the stock market without having to pay tax. Bearing in mind that normally you would have to pay tax on income – the income received from dividends – this is a major concession for taxpayers, particularly for those who want, say, to invest in income-generating unit trusts.

Furthermore, PEPs do not have to pay any capital gains tax – so for anyone wishing to dispose of their investments in a year when their CGT liability passes their personal allowance, then this concession is well worth having.

The tax concessions are particularly worthwhile for long-term savers. The ability to 'roll up' gross interest can have a major impact on the performance of a long-term savings scheme.

Since the 1989 Budget, there has been a massive outpouring of Personal Equity Plans from a wide range of financial institutions. The unit trust, and to a certain extent, the investment trust groups, who have a lot to gain by promoting PEPs, have been particularly active.

So what are the ground rules? Investors are allowed to put up to £4,800 into a PEP in any one tax year. If married and both husband and wife want a PEP then they can do so up to £9,600.

PEPs are designed to fuel the UK stock market, so your money must go into UK equities.

Of that £4,800, up to £2,400 can go into unit or investment

trusts, providing that the bulk of the underlying investment is in UK shares.

One of the problems facing the companies who provide PEPs is that of administration – particularly administering the purchase of shares. For stockbrokers and financial institutions used to handling share dealing, this is not too much of a problem, providing their office systems are okay.

But for some unit trust and investment trust company groups, the thought of having to administer the buying and selling of an individual's shares is something of a nightmare. Some groups have got around the problem by buying and managing blocks of shares and unit trusts on behalf of their customers.

This means that the investor effectively leaves the manager to get on with it – there is little choice in selecting your own shares. The big advantage here is that the scheme is cheaper than those whereby the investor has total control.

But even these managed schemes have not found favour with the bulk of the collective investment groups, and so they have found a way around the problem by not offering 'full' PEPs – that is, to allow the investor to put in the full £4,800, rather, they have gone for either unit trust or investment trust-only PEPs, allowing the client to invest up to £2,400, so taking up the full collective investment allowance.

This has not been too onerous a task for the collective investment groups, simply because they now only have to amend their systems to change the reporting procedure to the Inland Revenue. And while most full PEPs have to be paid for by the investor, most 'unit trust only' or 'investment trust only' PEPs do not cost the investor any more than would be paid for a straightforward unit or investment trust investment.

Why put PEP into your investments?

Putting PEP into your investment is therefore not such a bad idea – given the tax benefits. And if unit trust groups charge no more for buying units through a PEPs scheme, then you might as well do so to shelter yourself from any income tax payable on the dividends.

But there is more to Personal Equity Plans than simply vehicles through which to buy unit trusts. Remember way back in Chapter Two where we discussed your first investment – your house? I then mentioned the fact that PEPs can be used as a savings plan to pay off your mortgage.

Obviously a 'full' PEP in which you can put £4,800 in the 1989-90 tax year, is not such a good idea if you want to pay for your home because of the volatility of the shares element which consist of all or half the portfolio – the rest being made up of unit trusts.

But a unit trust or, indeed, an investment trust PEP, is better because share volatility is reduced as the underlying assets are spread among a larger number of companies.

Unit and investment trusts are, of course, subject to the fluctuations of the stock market as a whole, but bearing in mind that the life of a mortgage is usually 25 years, then this, too, helps iron-out fluctuations in the stock market over the long term.

Remember the figures I used when comparing the average performance of a unit trust in the UK General sector against the average endowment policy over 25 years? Just to remind you, having paid £30 a month, the average endowment would have paid out £43,911 while the average unit trust would have paid £86,126 – almost twice as much.

The point that has to be remembered here is that the unit trust's performance is based on the 'net' roll-up of interest, whereas under the PEP you would see the gross income reinvested.

So what difference does this 'grossing up' have on the performance of a unit trust? Well, £1,000 invested over five years would have grown to £2,579 over five years if net income had been reinvested, and £2,681 if gross income had been reinvested. So there is not a great deal of difference in the short term.

However, if you look at a 25-year period the net figure would have risen to £24,078, but the gross figure would have soared to £38,638, which is substantially higher.

Of course, past performance is no guide to the future, but given the 25-year time span of a mortgage you have to ask yourself is this really a great risk? And in answering that you must bear in mind inflation, particularly house price inflation, which effectively reduces the size of your loan in relation to your salary after such a long time span.

You would, therefore, have to be very cautious to accept that the traditional endowment offered greater safety, particularly when bonuses are not guaranteed!

But while PEP mortgages might sound a good idea, you could well find some resistance when trying to get one. Insurance companies pay huge commissions for agents who sell them while unit trust commissions are usually much lower. So the organization selling you the endowment has a particular interest in its sale.

PEP mortgages also have the great advantage over endowments of being more flexible. If, for example, your PEP investments had done very well over the first 15 years of their life, and their value matched the size of your loan, then there is no reason why you could not pay off your loan early.

You cannot easily do this with an endowment. Even if you could pay off your loan, you are still committed to your endowment policy even though you may prefer to cash it in.

The fact is that the surrender rate of endowment policies is very high; therefore, a more flexible repayment vehicle should be welcomed.

Now perhaps you can see why Mr Nigel Lawson created something of a revolution when he invented the Personal Equity Plan.

FOURTEEN

Higher Risk Investments

Options

While bank and building societies are at one end of a spectrum of risk, so options are at the other, principally because most people find them and the way they work so difficult to understand.

Combine a lack of knowledge with a failure to read the stock market correctly and your whole investment could be at serious risk. You therefore need to be an expert at following the market.

There are two types of option – 'traded options' and 'non-traded' options', both of which confer the right, once you have handed over your money, to either buy or sell a share at a given price within a given period.

They are a strange animal, because they offer the potential of huge capital gains for such a small outlay. It should be said then, that any investment that promises that is by its very nature risky.

You do not actually buy shares when you buy options; rather you buy contracts to buy or sell shares at a given price some time in the future.

Of the two types of option, the non-traded or traditional options are the easiest to explain.

They work like this: you invest your money into an options 'contract' which gives you the right to buy or sell at a given date for a given price. The price you pay represents a percentage of the share price of the company involved.

£1,000 invested in options might give you the right to buy ten times as many shares as you would have bought if you had decided to buy shares in the normal manner.

At the end of the set period – usually three months – if you had a call option to buy the shares at a certain price, then you would exercise it if it had reached its 'striking' price – a pre-determined price which was higher than the prevailing market price three months earlier.

The profit on the deal is, therefore, ten times greater than the profit gained from ordinary share dealing – once, of course, expenses had been deducted.

However, if the price did not reach the striking price, you would not want to exercise the contract so it would lapse, and you would lose all your money.

Of course, if you were confident that the share price was going to fall then you would buy a put option, and the procedure would work in reverse.

The difference between the 'traditional' option and the 'traded' option is that traded option contracts can be bought and sold. Therefore if, during the contract period, you saw that your contract was not going the way you had hoped then at least you could sell it to cut your losses.

As you can see, traded options are not for the faint-hearted! Your tactic, therefore, is to enlist the help of a stockbroker, or at the very least take time to write to the International Stock Exchange in London and ask for their guidebook on the subject.

The Business Expansion Scheme

The Business Expansion Scheme has been around for some time now, but it is really only worth considering if you are a higher rate taxpayer.

Indeed, the whole rationale of the scheme is to reward with tax concessions investors who take a high risk.

The tax relief is given at the outset, once the scheme has produced a tax certificate for the Inland Revenue. But beware: any delay in producing this certificate also means a delay in the payment of the tax relief.

BES is designed to provide capital for new companies, in the hope that they will grow into much bigger companies, providing their initial shareholders with a big increase in the value of their shares.

But the Inland Revenue says that you can only reap the benefits – particularly the capital gains – provided you hold the shares for a minimum of five years, and provided the company satisfies the requirements of the scheme during that time.

The type of BES scheme which you are most likely to come across these days is a new type of scheme, linked to the provision of rented housing. This new-style BES came about because of Government changes in the type of tenancy available to those who wished to rent homes.

'Assured tenancies' give a tenant security of tenure. Once a landlord has fixed a rent – which can increase with the rate of inflation – then the tenant's use of that property at that rent is 'assured'.

The only time the landlord can put up the rent, over and above the rate of inflation, is after one tenant moves out and another moves in and arranges a new agreement. Therefore it is in the interest of the landlord to get tenants who are unlikely to stay long, such as students, nurses etc.

BES schemes have been set up to exploit these new arrangements, and the BES companies aim at buying property in order to let them at a reasonable rent.

From the investor's point of view, the company makes money, firstly from rental income – which pays for its costs – and then over the long term from the appreciation in the value of the properties.

What has made BES-assured tenancy schemes particularly attractive is that you can invest a minimum of £500 in a company whose job is simply to invest in other BES companies involved in assured tenancy. By doing this, you effectively spread your money around in much the same way as you do with an investment trust. This reduces the high risk usually associated with investing in a single BES venture, which could range from schemes as diverse in their objectives as manufacturing or growing Christmas trees.

After five years, providing you have managed to stick to a whole set of the Inland Revenue's 'qualifying' rules, then if you want to sell your shares you can do so without having to pay either income or capital gains tax on them.

You can find BES funds through stockbrokers, through local business contacts, through the press or through specialist magazines set up to provide information on such schemes for would-be investors.

As with most investments, you would be well advised to seek advice on any scheme. Such is the nature of BES schemes that advice can be sought from a wide range of professionals – independent financial advisers, accountants and solicitors, for example.

Another provider of BES schemes is the Nationwide Anglia Building Society which operates one of the BES investment fund schemes, designed to spread your money around.

You can also get more information from the Government. If you live in Scotland, write to the Scottish Development Department, St Andrews House, Edinburgh EH1 3DE and ask for a copy of 'Assured Tenancies in Scotland – Your Rights and Responsibilities'. If you live anywhere else in the UK, write to the Department of the Environment, 2 Marsham Street, London SW1P 3EB and ask for a copy of 'The Assured Tenancy Scheme'.

Further help on assured tenancy can be found from your local Citizens Advice Bureau.

If you would prefer to look more generally at BES then get a copy of 'IR51: The Business Expansion Scheme', produced by the Inland Revenue and available from your local Inland Revenue office.

While most BES schemes are of high risk, because you just do not know how these usually new companies are going to fare, the risks can be reduced by the tried and tested method of spreading your money around.

Seek advice from specialists whose firms can usually be found in the specialist magazines.

The Unlisted Securities Market – and others

You will, no doubt, come across other types of investment which involve the purchase of shares.

The Unlisted Securities Market and the Third Market, both of which are likely to be merged, are more risky because these stock markets are markets devised to encourage the growth of small businesses.

However, from the investor's point of view, there is no 'scheme' whereby you can invest in these markets – you simply buy shares in the companies which trade on them.

The Unlisted Securities Market – the 'USM' – was created in 1980 by the main Stock Exchange to provide a market in the shares of companies who were less developed – in particular, companies who could not provide a proper five year trading record.

The USM imposes much less onerous regulations on USM companies in order to nurture them, hopefully for promotion to a 'full listing' some time in the future. Most of the companies we know – ICI, Hanson, GEC, Barclays – are all companies with a full listing.

The danger with dealing in USM or Third Market shares is that because many of them have not yet fully proved themselves, there is always the danger that some will go bust and you will lose your money. It is up to you whether you feel a company is good enough or not, and, again, professional advice from a stockbroker could save a lot of grief.

Useful Addresses

Age Concern England, 60 Pitcairn Road, Mitcham, Surrey CR4 3LL. Telephone (01) 640 5431

Age Concern Scotland, 33 Castle Street, Edinburgh EH2 3DN. Telephone (031) 225 5000

Age Concern Wales, 1 Park Grove, Cardiff, South Glamorgan CF1 3BJ. Telephone (0222) 371821/371566

Age Concern Northern Ireland, 6 Lower Crescent, Belfast BT7 1NR. Telephone (0232) 245729

Association of Futures Brokers and Dealers Ltd (AFBD), Plantation House, 5-8 Mincing Lane, London EC3M 3DX. Telephone (01) 626 9763

The Association of Investment Trust Companies, 6th floor, Park House, 16 Finsbury Circus, London EC2M 7JU. Telephone (01) 588 5347/8

Bonds and Stock Office, Marton, Blackpool FY3 9YP. Telephone (0253) 697333 – for Income Bonds and Government Stocks (Gilts)

Bonds and Stock Office, Government Buildings, Lytham St Annes FY0 1YN. Telephone (0253) 721212 – for Premium Bonds

British Insurance and Investment Brokers' Association, BIIBA House, 14 Bevis Marks, London EC3A 7NT. Telephone (01) 623 9043

Building Societies Association, 3 Savile Row, London W1X 1AF. Telephone (01) 437 0655

Building Societies Ombudsman, 35-37 Grosvenor Gardens, London SW1X 7AW. Telephone (01) 931 0044

Citizens Advice Bureaux:
The National Association of Citizens Advice Bureaux, Myddelton House, 115-123 Pentonville Road, London N1 9LZ. Telephone (01) 833 2181

The Scottish Association of Citizens Advice Bureaux, 26 George Square, Edinburgh EH8 9LD. Telephone (031) 667 0156/8

The Northern Ireland Association of Citizens Advice Bureaux, New Forge Lane, Belfast BT9 5NW. Telephone (0232) 681117

Department of the Environment, 2 Marsham Street, London SW1P 3EB. Telephone (01) 276 3000 and ask for the public enquiries unit

Financial Intermediaries, Managers and Brokers Regulatory Association (FIMBRA), 22 Great Tower Street, London EC3R 5AQ. Telephone (01) 538 8860

Investment Management Regulatory Organization (IMRO), Centrepoint, 103 New Oxford Street, London WC1A 1PT. Telephone (01) 379 0601

Life Assurance and Unit Trust Regulatory Organization (LAUTRO), Centrepoint, 103 New Oxford Street, London WC1A 1QW. Telephone (01) 379 0444

National Savings, Durham, DH99 1NS.
Write to the above for information about certificates, yearly
plans and SAYE

National Savings, Glasgow, G58 1SB.
Write to the above for information about ordinary and
investment accounts and deposit bonds

For further information about all National Savings products,
telephone (01) 605 9461; (0253) 723714; or (041) 632 2766

Scottish Development Department:
Scottish Office, St Andrews House, Edinburgh, EH1 3DE.
Telephone (031) 556 8400 or Dover House, Whitehall,
London SW1A 2AU. Telephone (01) 270 3000

Securities and Investment Board, 3 Royal Exchange Buildings,
London EC3V 3NL. Telephone (01) 283 2474

The Society of Pension Consultants, Ludgate House, Ludgate
Circus, London EC4A 2AB. Telephone (01) 353 1688

The Stock Exchange. Throgmorton Street, London EC2N
1HP. Telephone (01) 588 2355

The Securities Association, The Stock Exchange, London
EC2N 1EQ. Telephone (01) 588 2355

Unit Trust Association, 65 Kingsway, London WC2B 6TD.
Telephone (01) 831 0895

Unit Trust Ombudsman, 31 Southampton Row, London
WC1B 5HJ. Telephone (01) 242 8613